SHERBORNE

An Experiment in Transformation

SHERBORNE

An Experiment in Transformation

ALLEN ROTH

Bennett Books
Santa Fe, New Mexico

Bennett Books
P.O. Box 1553
Santa Fe, New Mexico 87504

Printed in the United States of America
02 01 00 99 98   5 4 3 2 1

Book design: Amara Projansky
Cover Design: Amara Projansky
Cover Photos: J.G. Bennett, 1973 © Annette Green;
Sherborne Gate, compliments The Sherborne Trust
Dedication page photo: Compliments of Laurence Sutton

Library of Congress Cataloging-in-Publication Data
Roth, Allen, 1943-
Sherborne: an experiment in transformation / Allen Roth
p.   cm.
Includes index.
ISBN 1-881408-09-4 (alk. paper)
1. Bennett, John G. (John Godolphin), 1897-1974. 2. Roth, Allen, 1943- .
3.Sherborne Academy for Continuous Education--Biography.
I. Title.
BP610.B462R68   1998
299'.93--dc21
[B]   98-39694
CIP

Limited Cloth Edition: ISBN 1-881408-10-8

CONTENTS

List of Photographs viii

Acknowledgments ix

Introduction 1

CHAPTERS ~

ONE My side of the story 3

TWO Michael handed me a folded pamphlet 7

THREE A word about John Bennett is in order 9

FOUR In late August, 1971 16

FIVE The first officially scheduled event 22

SIX Much of the teaching at Sherborne 27

SEVEN The fire was going 44

EIGHT We distinguished sensation from feeling 49

~ photographs ~

NINE Mr. Holland taught Fourth Way psychology 63

TEN Instructions to cooperate 67

ELEVEN I heard it said of the First Obligatory 72

TWELVE Anna Durco was a contained mandarin presence . . 77

THIRTEEN One morning I met Bennett 84

FOURTEEN There were several other specialists 88

FIFTEEN "I can serve as an example for you" 94

SIXTEEN The "Purgatory" chapter of *Beelzebub's Tales* 97

SEVENTEEN By February everyone knew each other 100

EIGHTEEN It is said that we cannot see 109

NINETEEN The last afternoon of my year at Sherborne 114

Index 119

LIST OF PHOTOGRAPHS

Mr. B and Mick Sutton viii

CENTERPAGES:

Elizabeth Bennett; Bhante; Virgil Walker; Gerald Wilde 55

Images of J.G. Bennett 56

Movements Performances at Sherborne House 57

Movements Performance & Students 58

Passover, Students, Lili Helstinius 59

Miss Olga de Nottbeck, Enneagram Rose Garden 60

Dining Room, Gerald Wilde; George Cornelius & Gerald Green . . 61

The Bennetts; Tony Blake; Laurence & Michael Sutton 62

~ all photographs are courtesy of Virgil Walker except where noted.

ACKNOWLEDGMENTS

This book has been fleshed out by two surprise contributions, the journal of fellow student Lynn O'Brien (Quirolo), and an evocative memoir of Michael Sutton by his wife, Laurence. I am grateful to them for sharing their personal experiences, and to Anna Durco, for consenting to let my characterization of her stand basically as I first wrote it. Likewise to the others who appear in the story, whose names are withheld.

Thanks to Brent Daniel and Anthony Blake, my first readers, for prodding me whenever I bogged down; to Rachel Altman who first saw how to make the material into a whole; to Hugh Elliot for his sound instinct and sense of humor; and particularly to my publisher, James Tomarelli, for his patience.

While paring the book down to size, some contributors have gone unmentioned, such as artist-psychologist Edith Wallace, group-dynamics specialist Tony Hodgson, and Pierre Elliot, the future director of an American offshoot of the Sherborne experiment.

Special thanks to Virgil Walker, another fellow Sherborne graduate. We have become cracker-barrel philosophers; his honest appraisals of the book, of Sherborne itself, and of ourselves then and today, has helped me take a more impartial view of what I was saying, and not saying. Walker, now a first-rate sculptor, has taught me patience for a slow-moving task, by watching him at work.

To Betty H. Roth, my wife, who co-authored this with her own consistent clarity. We discovered each other and married, some years after she herself attended the fifth and last Sherborne course.

To my daughter, Olivia and my son, Jonas, for whom this book has really been written. May it remind both of you to appreciate this life.

Last but not least, to the English people and their hospitality. No place on Earth could have accommodated the Sherborne experiment with such aplomb and conviviality toward the eccentric.

—Allen Roth
Scottsdale, Arizona
June, 1998

© Laurence Sutton

"Mr B" and Mick Sutton
Sherborne House, 1972

Dedicated to the memory of
J.G. Bennett and Michael Sutton.

"Sometimes a thing is disguised by appearing to be exactly what it is."

INTRODUCTION

This book tells of a little-known experiment in psychological and spiritual education that took on the form of an Academy. Open to any willing candidate, regardless of their preparation or background, the curriculum was conceived and executed by British philosopher and teacher, John G. Bennett, in the last years of his life. I was among the ninety people who attended the first of these ten-month courses at Sherborne House, in England, 1971-72.

John Bennett is remembered foremost for his association with the Gurdjieff-Ouspensky circle, an influential philosophical movement in Europe and America, that reached its zenith in public awareness back in the 1920s and 30s. This irregular organization of ideas and practices in self-study became forgotten in the wake of World War II.

Forgotten, but not entirely. From the time of its appearance in the West, the universality of this "fourth way" teaching continued to draw interested persons to the few quasi-clandestine groups dedicated to putting its ideas into practice. Among these study groups were John Bennett's own long-standing circle of pupils and associates. Bennett came to regard their work together as part of a fifty-year incubation period, where the results upon people of this unique psychological teaching could be observed.

Bennett developed his own understanding of the ideas of Gurdjieff and Ouspensky, and applied them in scientific and pedagogic contexts throughout his life. This line of work culminated in his founding the Sherborne Academy for Continuous Education as a response to the numbers of enthusiastic new people, mostly young adults, English and American, emerging from the unsettling events of the 1960s.

Although Sherborne alumni themselves, when asked, will typically testify to its profound impact on their lives, no general account or memoir of these courses as they experienced them has appeared thus far. In terms of public awareness, the experiment may as well have never existed.

This left me with an open field when I found myself writing this book, two decades after my own, as it were, "graduation." It has taken me much time to complete this book. In the process, I wrote two kinds of books: the first, in a pseudo-detached, third-person style; the second, a subjective, involved, first-person account, which gradually supplanted the former. I am indebted to early readers who noted that Sherborne came alive only in the retelling of personal experiences, and not in my rehash of ideas or the substance of Mr. Bennett's talks. These latter, in any case, can be found elsewhere.

Hence, readers will find little in the way of theory or specialized terminology. I apologize outright if I leave an interested outsider, on whom this book is focused, guessing at the meaning of a word or reference. I have relied on ordinary language wherever I could, and defined special terms when they could not be avoided. The result is, I hope, a flowing narrative which does not bog down with superfluous discussion. I want to leave the reader with an impression of an extraordinarily unified, year-long event.

—Allen Roth
Scottsdale, Arizona
June, 1998

CHAPTER ~ ONE

MY SIDE OF the story of the International Academy for Continuous Education, more commonly remembered by its alumni as Sherborne House, began in India, 1969. There, in a village called Mehrauli, I met a Londoner who poured into my ear stories of a charismatic English philosopher and teacher, the circle of people he attracted around him, and their center for study and work called Coombe Springs. Michael Sutton was one of the latter day set who frequented the center in the 50's, before it was disbanded in an extravagant, symbolic gesture. What I heard from Michael convinced me that there was an original and self-sustaining offshoot of an obscure spiritual tradition I had read about avidly, sought for in America, and now, without much logic, was seeking in the East.

I was twenty-seven when I left the States with a half-year's supply of money. (At that time one could board a charter flight from LAX to Gatwick for a couple hundred dollars.) To travel overland through Europe and the Near East during those years was to plunge into a broad, slow-moving river composed chiefly of the newly-arisen Hippie Internationale, Americans on grand tour and Europeans on extended holiday, all with their itinerant hustlers, junkies, penniless expatriates, and seekers-of gurus, ways, religion, drugs, sex, adventure, the miraculous.

I happened to end up in a youth hostel south of New Delhi, a Buddhist mission which provided floor space inside a pavilion of scalloped archways and open nooks. The pavilion was centered like a simple jewel in a walled acreage—an old Mogul pleasure garden converted to farmland. The stone walls, twenty feet high, were breached by two opposing gatehouses, containing rooms stacked on either side of their tall, central portals. An Indian family of squatters occupied the gatehouse facing the road. The gatehouse opposite, unoccupied, opened onto a circuitous footpath through overgrown ruins into the water-blessed village of Mehrauli. The village was the ancient site of Delhi, "Number Two" of the five consecutive cities bearing that name over the years into modern times. Rumor had it that the mission was entrusted to an old monk who dwelled somewhere within the precincts of the shrine at the end of a long central path. The monk was seldom seen. Every morning an Englishman, who apparently worked for him, amiably collected our rupees, then disappeared. The place was unsupervised, save for a zany sweeper called Bagal, who hustled *bakshish* by pantomime.

At night the doorless niches became candlelit conversation pits. Chilums of hashish were passed around and everyone partook. Swapping adventures and survival tips provided the entertainment and a way of attaining status. One convivial evening I retold Gurdjieff's slapstick version of the Greek and Roman foundations of modern civilization, which he calls with mock solemnity in his book, *Beelzebub's Tales to His Grandson,* "The Fruits of Former Civilizations and the Blossoms of the Contemporary." One of our little group then told me that, apropos of Gurdjieff, only yesterday he spoke with some sort of "dancing teacher," who presumably resided somewhere on the property. He was unable to tell me who he was or how he could be found, but the following morning a new face turned up to collect our rupees. He appeared to be Muslim, perhaps a Turk, with a lambs wool cap and mustache. But there was something Dickensian about him: shoulder-length, black-brown hair, the sweater one size too small, the darting entrance and the mischievous, tarsier-like gaze. His Surrey accent completed the effect.

In the midst of his jubilant bantering, which captured the attention of everyone, he seemed to be throwing out little hints which I found myself understanding. This must be the mystery man, the "dancing teacher," I realized. I said something about "shachermacher workshops," an insider's expression for sham study groups. Michael Sutton grinned his display of neglected teeth and said, "We need to talk." And so we did, all that night on the roof of a ruined temple just beyond the mission walls, and throughout the months I remained at Asoka Vihara.

Michael was a fantastic weaver of stories. He conjured the long, erratic history of Coombe Springs, and the extreme mental and physical commitment placed on its membership, under the direction of a tireless, gifted, overachieving torchbearer-whom Michael affectionately referred to as "B."

No repository of orthodox tradition, Coombe Springs. No jumping through hoops to get past the door. Newcomers either recoiled at the demands placed on them, or welcomed them as means for putting certain psycho-spiritual ideas to the test. By this osmosis, Coombe Springs became more than a center for study; it was a caravan attempting to keep stride with a long-legged scout who had no clear idea where he was going. By intuition and faith, he changed direction many times along the way.

I found Michael's verbal portraits of life at Coombe Springs immensely appealing. I was of the opinion that people are more likely to season spiritually under extreme and disorderly conditions than tidy, stable ones. Had Coombe Springs still existed, I would have made a beeline for the front gate. But it all came to an end when their impulsive leader, J.G. Bennett, persuaded the membership to give the property and its fixtures away, no strings attached. The recipient was the Sufi teacher, Idries Shah.

It was Bennett's last act as leader of a community. He withdrew himself from that role into a sort of private life, leaving his long-time pupils and co-workers to make their way alone. Michael was one of these: former Coombe Springs kitchen manager and part-time court jester, he had recently been invited to India to meet a remarkable Cambodian Buddhist Mahathera, the Venerable Vira Dharmawara.

ASOKA VIHARA WAS THE FINAL DESTINATION of one-way Eurasian bus tours, solely managed by another Coombe Springs veteran, Brian Page. Brian's motley band of passengers were unfailingly relieved at entering this island of peace amidst the jarring ambiance of India. The temperature of the compound was consistently several degrees warmer in winter and as many degrees cooler in the summer. Brian convinced his friend Michael to join this latest tour. After their passengers disembarked, Brian sold the tour bus in Nepal, as usual, and both of them were now earning their keep by helping manage the mission.

Bhante, as the Venerable Vira Dharmawara was known to those close to him, welcomed me kindly into his tiny community. I moved out of the pavilion into one of the rooms constructed near the shrine. An ancient, reclusive Swiss woman, named Madam Jane, had been occupying one of the quarters for years. Michael and Brian were in the next set of rooms down, then there was mine which I shared with two Englishmen-seasoned India travelers I had met in Lahore.

The monk had in his charge two grandchildren: Phobal, a twenty-year old woman, just admitted to Friends World College; and Ôn, her brother, about thirteen. With an ever changing little circle of hangers-on, Bhante shared his hours for meditation—even his breakfast and noon meals, which Michael and the quiet Mehrauli woman, Parvati, prepared in his kitchen. Otherwise the monk left us to ourselves, while conducting his affairs through correspondence and by sojourns outside the country. His presence could be felt everywhere. Round, handsome and head shorn, a pair of missing teeth completed his resemblance to a laughing Buddha. His amused, hooded eyes were those of a dignitary; he had been a judge, later a provincial governor—the first Cambodian native to be appointed so under French rule. A large crayfish tattoo on his golden forearm occasionally flashed out from under his cloak.

This man of eighty years glowed with a deep-sourced kindness for everyone who came within his sphere. To sit at table with him was like basking in the sun. He made himself available to anyone who came to him with needs, physical or otherwise. But he had few illusions about people. To the bands of westerners passing through the mission during those high flown years, he was unfailingly respectful and kind; privately he doubted their presumed virtues. "Hippie-crites," he chortled. Behind this melodious laughter was a knowing and canny customer.

Asoka Vihara had been entrusted to Bhante by Prime Minister Nehru as a hospice for sick Tibetan refugees pouring into New Delhi after the Chinese takeover. The Vihara, or mission, now subsisted independently through the sale of vegetable crops the resident farmer coaxed from the land, and the daily yield of the youth hostel: one rupee—ten cents U.S. on the black market—multiplied by an average eighteen lodgers.

Dharmawara never inquired about the spiritual training Michael Sutton received in England, or for that matter, my own obvious interest in it. He did recognize in Michael a rare and special insight and a gift for drawing people's attention toward the cosmic fun around them. Dharmawara approved; but with unspoken reservation about Michael's appetite for the experiential. What could be done? he projected silently. All these young Westerners seemed determined nowadays to waste themselves with drugs.

He accepted me as one who was searching for real understanding. I was becoming, however, less sure of what I was searching for. I had come upon a man who could help me on that search but I could not picture myself taking on his discipline, the monk's way of renunciation.

I was not so much desiring enlightenment, if indeed I even believed in such a thing, as simply wishing to become functional. That accounts for my attraction to Gurdjieffian philosophy, which starts from that very position. It spoke in the only language which had any force for me. "I have very good leather to sell to those who want to make shoes out of it," Gurdjieff said, indicating a pragmatism that set his ideas apart from other esoteric or religious traditions.

Although it was a pragmatism declaring indebtedness to all the oldest religions and traditions, for me it was not a way that could translate into or be substituted by another way. When it comes to religion, form is just as essential as the content. I was not interested in escaping from the coils of the world of illusion, although I saw the point. Rather I wanted to come to terms with *that* world, for it is the one I am cast into. I wanted to learn how to play the hand that was dealt to me.

But Coombe Springs was dead and gone. There was perhaps one option open to me: to imbibe the influence of the venerable monk. Michael and I sometimes speculated on the possibility of another work community springing up in the Vihara. With this fantasy in mind, I left for the States, and then returned the following year to the mission with Sally, my first wife.

Bhante welcomed us newlyweds warmly, quartered us next to the shrine, and—as with Brian and Michael—gave us work helping with the affairs of the mission. Both of them had departed, months before my return. Brian was back in London. Michael had gone north into Kashmir, then parts west—it was rumored.

This second journey was confirmation of an old truth: that we cannot step twice into the same river. A sense of being out of place gradually settled in. I felt coarse and earthbound, too dense for the rarefied peace of the mission. I became restless, needing to make something out of what I perceived was a narrowing field of choices. I confessed all this to Sally. We soon agreed to pay our respects to Bhante and take our leave. We traveled for a while, then drove back to Amsterdam to sell our van and book a flight out of London for home.

With two free days in London before our departure to the States, I rang up Robin, one of Michael's old friends, to see if he had news of him. Robin, quite surprised, told us that Michael had just arrived at his flat, unannounced. When we knocked at Robin's door an hour later, a bearded Michael Sutton saluted us with sly glee. "I said to Robin after you rang up, 'Well now, there's two more for the course!'"

CHAPTER ~ TWO

MICHAEL HANDED ME a folded pamphlet, a prospectus for something called The International Academy for Continuous Education, which we read standing while he made a telephone call. It quickly dawned on me that it was written by Bennett.

> *This prospectus is addressed to those who care about the future-their own and that of mankind: especially those who have already searched and experimented with politics, social service, those who have looked for new experience in travel, in sex or in drugs, for those who have tried religion or plunged into one of the many "isms" and movements that promise a new world, and have found them all lacking in an essential ingredient: that is practicality. On every hand there are people to tell us what we ought to do, but few indeed have any idea how to do it. The basic course of the International Academy for Continuous Education is designed primarily for the purpose of teaching men and women of all ages how to live their lives in the way they themselves wish. It is particularly directed to those who are acutely aware of an unrealized self, of energies squandered and of time wasted-who are prepared to go through hard training in order to change. It is, above all, for those who have realized that the "first step in helping the world is to help oneself," that inner change must come before outer change.*

Meanwhile, Michael was speaking with John Bennett's wife, Elizabeth, about an American couple on their way back from India—potential candidates for the new school. Michael waited in silence for a minute until she returned to the phone, saying that Bennett wanted to meet us, and that he would be available this afternoon.

Robin drove us to the Bennett home, at the end of a cul-de-sac in Kingston-Upon-Thames. Next to the house was a low-slung outbuilding with a nameplate, Coombe Springs Press. A gray-eyed woman, Elizabeth Bennett, saw us arriving through the window of the print shop, removed her printer's apron, and met us out on the path. She spoke few words, but pleasantly escorted us into the house, seated us in a comfortable parlor and left us there to find "Mr. B."

After some minutes, a man walked into the room, filling it with a large presence. Well into his seventies, six and a half feet tall, he reminded me of a leaner version of Harold Macmillan. His face was more angular, with thin hair and mustache gone nearly white. His eyes emitted little sparks, suffusing the impression of a flash going off. The effect spoke of his energy. He was very urbane, observing courtesies while finding a new seating arrangement for us. He sat with his back to a window looking out on the street. His eyes closed momentarily, and we sat in silence. His shoulders went slack. This reminded me to relax.

He parceled out his conversation mostly from behind closed eyes, as if he were bringing an interior object into focus. When the words became unlocked and started to flow, his face opened into a beaming smile, icy, kind eyes on mine, until he closed himself around his next words. He gave the impression of a diver resurfacing, making contact, and descending again to retrieve the next piece of cargo.

He needed very little information about us. We had traveled in Asia on a search, had learned of him through Michael. We had read most of the teaching's source material. We wanted to know about the new school. He wanted to know if we were willing to commit to a year of uninterrupted work, in a communal social arrangement. He gave us some copies of the prospectus and asked us to let people at home know that this experiment was taking place. We agreed, thanked him, and left. I already trusted him: he was confident, supremely competent, and intent on doing something useful. The meeting was absurdly brief, as if it were a foregone conclusion of events we unknowingly had participated in.

This specter of confidence and competence had just returned from a hastily improvised itinerary of speaking engagements in England and America. What his audiences, mainly college students, heard was a severe criticism of modern education, which in his view did nothing to prepare people for the extreme changes occurring everywhere in the world. The academy he was founding was an experimental approach to this educational deficiency. Those who were prepared to commit themselves to a year of hard work were asked to arrange to speak with him privately after the lecture.

The school year was just ending, and many were already in the process of returning home for the summer. In spite of the last minute notice and no previous publicity, a total of ninety people, some with families, signed on and showed up for the first year.

Two-thirds of those people were Americans; nearly the rest were British. Sixty-six of the student body were under twenty-five. Many had just graduated, not yet committed to jobs, careers or graduate studies. They came, for the most part, from middle or upper middle class society; several came from the trades and professions; a few were retired or pensioned—the eldest being in his eighties.

Many of them knew little or nothing of Gurdjieff and Company, and Bennett made it clear this might be to their special advantage. It was Bennett himself who appeared to have grasped the situation and was offering something called practicality. The events of the sixties had cast doubt on our civil institutions, our future, perhaps even our own collective sanity. Bennett's claim that we can actually learn to live as we would wish to live was persuasive. That it came from a seventy-four-year-old untenured philosopher, added credibility.

CHAPTER ~ THREE

A WORD ABOUT J.G. (John Godolphin) Bennett is in order as Sherborne House—the school, that is—would not have existed without him.

He must have come into this world with a sense of self-destiny. He was endowed with enough brains and native sense to rise to influence in more than one field of industry and scientific research, without obtaining much in the way of a professional pedigree. His autobiography, *Witness,** an account of his spiritual and public life, is an oddly revealing combination of sincerity, candor, and self-promotion. When I first read it, I could not tell if all of its negative self-portrayal was intentional.

His intelligence and capabilities, however, credited the causes he championed. His way of taking a good idea seriously inspired the lives of hundreds of different people who met him. Bennett's worldly credentials, not unlike those of Rudolph Steiner, satisfied my own conception of the Renaissance Hero. He has been remembered as a metaphysical philosopher, but I think now he was an equally gifted psychologist. To be associated with this polymath guru appealed to my vanity. "None of us can resist the temptation to make ourselves appear interesting," he pleads in the foreword to *Witness.* "There is no doubt that I have succumbed."

BENNETT GREW TO manhood during the dissolution of the European empires, of which he was sometimes a minor player. If his spiritual testimony glamorized, it could not be avoided. His life was rich in experience and productivity. He was driven by a need to continually outdo himself. His long career as an over-achieving student of spiritual awakening presented a sort of paradox for those who followed him. He made things happen, which is why many people looked to him as a source of help.

Bennett received the sort of education accorded to the upper classes. He was descendent of the "king-maker," Neville, Earl of Warwick, on his father's side. The greatest parental influence, however, seems to have come from his mother, an American of New England Puritan descent and temperament. She was attentive and caring of her three children, but aloof, coolly intellectual, repelled by outward displays of affection. She never understood Bennett's pursuit of the inner life, nor his indifference to achieving worldly success.

* *Witness: The Story of a Search.* Santa Fe: Bennett Books, 1998.

He graduated from Oxford in mathematics and chemistry, which helped inform his philosophical as well as his professional productivity. He played a role in diplomatic negotiations from time to time. Ramsay McDonald offered him a position in the Labour Party, but a career in politics, which more than once was opened to him, was never pursued. The persuasiveness and clarity of his ideas brought him an appointment as Director of Research into innovative use and delivery of coal power, England's primary energy source during World War II.

WITNESS BEGINS IN a field hospital in 1918, where young Bennett lay comatose from shrapnel wounds. He reports that a conscious part of him separated from his body and remained cognizant of conversations during his surgery and in the ward while recovering—a period of six days and nights. Some events he recollected were confirmed by the astonished staff nursing him back to life. The experience revealed to him that his connection with a physical body, and with death itself, was a complete mystery, marking for him the actual beginning of his life.

After convalescing in England, he was assigned as Acting Liaison Officer of the Turkish War Office during the disarmament. The post placed him at the center of British Intelligence activity in Istanbul, where he learned to speak Turkish and established many contacts that would shape his future.

Among the many post-war refugees coming into his sphere were the Russian writer Ouspensky and a circle of Russian émigrés, all somehow connected with an obscure Levantine of uncertain political leanings, whose dossier was in Bennett's files.

Bennett was introduced to this man, G.I. Gurdjieff, by a Turkish Prince who cultivated Bennett's growing interest in transcendental experience. This initial meeting with Gurdjieff made a vivid and long-lasting impression on him. The man was uncannily lucid on a range of subjects that, in ordinary circles, remain only speculative. After Bennett returned to England, he linked up with Ouspensky who was now teaching Gurdjieff's ideas and a new method for self-development, calling itself the "Fourth Way" or, as it was called by its practitioners, "the Work."

Ouspensky's lectures were then attracting the attention of writers and psychologists. Bennett absorbed the complex ideas rapidly and, showing himself an exceptional communicator, was asked to introduce newcomers to the basics. This thrust him into the position of teacher, a role that would be repeatedly projected onto him, one which he was never inclined to refuse. He continued his association with Ouspensky, eventually finding himself surrounded with people interested in working with him directly, especially after Ouspensky moved to America in 1941.

It was that same year that Bennett was authorized to locate suitable quarters for research laboratories. He found a seven-acre property, near Kingston Hill, called Coombe Springs, having an ample, but neglected, residence and several outbuildings needing repair. There were kitchen gardens and a fish pond to be rejuvenated. All of this was more or less available for occupation, separate from the laboratory itself and its needs. When the lease ran out after the war, the community, under registry as The Institute for the Comparative Study of History, Philosophy and the Sciences, Ltd., purchased it outright.

Bennett began an ambitious philosophical treatise, *The Dramatic Universe,* which made use of work ideas and terminology. Word got back to Ouspensky, who had definite views on bastardizing the teaching He promptly forbade all of his students to communicate with Bennett or his associates under any circumstances.

This independence of mind was what initially attracted me to Bennett. I was of the opinion that it was a necessary ingredient for appreciating Gurdjieff's ideas in the first place, designed as they are for being seen anew. How counter-productive it must have struck Bennett, to sequester his developing understanding year after year within Ouspensky's tight-handed censure.

The Dramatic Universe is the product of an ambidextrous thinker, versed in non-Euclidean geometry, steeped in Aristotle. Inspired by his near-death experience and subsequent insights which visited him, he maps the working of an interactive dimension between the conditions of time and space and a field of potentiality which he calls "eternity." This arcane groundwork is bolstered by a "Unified Field Theory in a Curvature-free Five-Dimensional Manifold," fleshed out by Bennett and two Cambridge mathematicians, with critical attention from Max Born. It was later accepted and published in the prestigious Proceedings of the Royal Society in 1949.

The framework for his arguments is a system of multi-termed models for taking concepts from (abstract) unity to succeeding levels of (concrete) multiplicity. The models themselves become one of the main concerns of the whole discourse, a methodology for objectifying things and situations of all descriptions.Called Systematics, this model, being a progression of discrete steps from abstract to concrete, has been adopted as a planning tool for the research and development divisions of a few leading industries.

Taken as a whole, however, *The Dramatic Universe* is a distinct departure from the customary fare of modern philosophy. It proceeds to map in detail vast speculative tracts of the noumenal world, unsupported by any authority other than the author's confidence in his own insight and in what he frankly asserts has been revealed to him. In academic circles he is regarded as that suspicious mix of philosopher and mystic, and the work has been predictably neglected.

AFTER THE WAR Bennett and his people made contact in Paris with Gurdjieff himself, where much of the theory which Ouspensky taught was immediately elevated to direct, personal experience. But a year or so following, Gurdjieff was dead, leaving behind him an organization in complete disarray. In perfect character, he had produced the conditions for conflict and friction by privately appointing several of his followers, including Bennett, to overlapping responsibilities.

By some understanding with Jeanne de Salzmann and other Gurdjieff Society leaders in Paris, Coombe Springs continued on as a center for study and practice, intermittently supported by the Paris group that had worked with Gurdjieff's movements and inner exercises for decades. Bennett published books, lectured, traveled, studied the source materials of other traditions, and sought out men and women who had seriously devoted their lives to awakening to reality. His years in Istanbul had put him in contact with several dervish communities, while his contacts in Western scientific circles were as fortuitous. With the publication of the first volume of *The Dramatic Universe,* his reputation began to cohere. When pressed to state his vocation, he replied, "philosopher." His students remained with him over the years, even during a period when he broke with Work discipline altogether.

This break developed after he was introduced in the 1950s to Subud, a spiritual practice which was attracting followers beyond the borders of Indonesia. Subud is a form of inner submission which opens one to a purifying spiritual action, transmitted from one person to another, with little or no preparation. Bennett experimented and became convinced that it was a force of great significance for mankind, and he directed his energy and the resources of Coombe Springs to assisting in its transmission. Bennett's relaxed and eloquent manner of explaining metaphysical concepts in a public forum, dispelling controversy and suspicion effortlessly, was an invaluable tool for a proliferating movement. He wrote books on the subject. He lectured and traveled, initiated many into the fold, and became a leading spokesman in the West for this new spiritual phenomenon. Following the advice of the founder, Pak Subuh, never to mix Subud practice with another discipline, he put an end to Fourth Way practice. He remembered Gurdjieff intimating that his teaching was preparatory to some later development. Subud very well may have been this new stage in the spiritualization of the world. At least that is how Bennett felt about it.

The first version of *Witness* ends here. He would update it, a number of years after his break with Subud, and after a succession of other influences converging at Coombe Springs.

The about-turns in Bennett's career illustrates the man. His sense of destiny in being in the midst of an unfolding scenario gave rise to impulsive actions which he would later modify or recant. After some years as a prominent spokesman for Subud, he began to have second thoughts about his inner life. He had been unquestionably transformed into another man: he remembered how excessively intellectual he was, how inclined to cold-heartedness. He had inherited his mother's trait of bearing little sympathy with people's frivolity and weaknesses. All this was changed in Bennett by the action of the latihan—the central practice of the Subud experience—which had the effect, as I heard him express it, of making him "practically human." Yet something essential had the appearance of withering; the total reliance upon the latihan was producing, he thought, a flaccid inner condition. The lack of personal effort seemed to be the cause of this sense of loss, and personal effort was the remedy. He and a number of old students began to meet again to take up the practice of the Fourth Way, while mixing in the latihan as they saw fit. This was loudly protested by those who took Pak Subuh's injunctions to heart. Subud's foremost publicist and promoter, during its rapid advancement in the West, was now its betrayer. For the second time in his life, he was in the position of a pariah.

Coombe Springs reformed itself again as a sort of laboratory for psycho-spiritual investigation. Bennett improvised and nurtured an ever-changing curriculum out of which came new and original material, published under the titles: *Energies, Material, Vital, and Cosmic,* and *A Spiritual Psychology.** These productive years also saw the completion of the final volumes of *The Dramatic Universe,* in which a circle of gifted younger minds participated, notably the author Anthony (A. G. E.) Blake, who was assigned sections to draft or finish outright in his own language.

Then, almost like clockwork, came another disruption, which marked the end of Coombe Springs. A Cambridge-educated Afghan Sufi, Idries Shah, threw out bait for the Gurdjieffians in the form of a pseudonymous travel article, offhandedy describing an apparatus seen in a mountain monastery, which models the postures and movements of ancient temple dances, reminiscent to any reader of *Meetings with Remarkable Men.* Shah later admitted to writing the article.

For Gurdjieff followers, this was hard to ignore. One of the ingenious devices of Gurdjieff's teaching was the deliberate ambiguity of origins, which point everywhere at once and nowhere in particular. The teaching is rooted in the past and at home with present understanding of the physical world, from universal expansion to plate tectonics. It echoes many traditions, from the Protestant work ethic to the Zervan heresy, yet remains apart from them all.

Shah claimed real knowledge of its origins. A colleague from British Intelligence days named Reggie Hoare ferreted out the author and reportedly said to Bennett that Shah demonstrated knowledge of a key component, the enneagram, surpassing anything Ouspensky ever knew. This was a claim without substance, but his credibility with Bennett was not founded there. After some reluctance from his first meeting with Shah, Bennett came to the conclusion that he indeed belonged to a tradition wherein the Fourth Way was rooted, and that he must assist Shah in his future work. He persuaded the Board of Directors to assign their beloved Coombe Springs to Shah who, upon hearing this offer, insisted that no strings be attached whatsoever and that the transaction must proceed without delay. An uncompromising break from the past and complete freedom in his disposition of the gift were his only terms. No guarantee to establish a center for Sufi studies was mentioned.

Coombe Springs was given over to Shah, as well as all the study groups that had formed around Bennett over the years. About half of the three-hundred or so people found some connection with Shah and his work; the rest were left in the air. Bennett himself was given no role in the new order. Before the year 1966 was

* to be re-printed in 1999 by Bennett Books.

out, Coombe Springs was put up for sale and Shah relocated his headquarters to Kent. There was no room for regret; this extravagant gesture had its own logic. The fate of the property, for good or ill, was out of Bennett''s hands. (It was subdivided for the development and sale of twenty-eight luxury homes.) Left with no responsibilities toward anyone, Bennett immersed himself in private affairs, no longer the teacher.

THE DIVESTITURE OF Coombe Springs would have been the demise of Bennett's Institute, had it not found new direction in a collaboration between Bennett and some younger students on a new project.

Bennett himself was invited to join a committee of the local power distributor, General Electric Company, which was charged with discovering why industry engineers, released for technical courses by their employers, were getting so little benefit from their training. Their study concluded that technical courses which focus on pre-determined operations and results, neglect the fact that most real engineering challenges are singularly open-ended. Bennett and his people launched a "deconditioning course" to follow the regular training sessions, with excellent results. Unfortunately, the deconditioning process required skilled tutors. Bennett's people could demonstrate it, but their energy was needed elsewhere, namely, in mechanizing the process. The joint effort resulted in a prototype of a user-driven teaching machine, called "Systemaster." Younger people, still wanting to work next to him, were set to developing and writing collateral teaching materials.

IBM became interested in Systemaster as a key to computerized education. A contract with the U.S. Navy was even in the making. But the ascent of a new administration to the White House resulted in budgetary cuts that affected many research programs in American industry. Among the casualties was Bennett's own project. He eventually sold the rights to a company interested in its industrial applications, rather than Bennett's objective of reforming education.

Out of this came fresh and useful contacts for Bennett. He was subsequently invited to give a seminar on his own methods for systems analysis, "Systematics," to a group of interested research-and-development engineers and production managers. The seminar was arranged by a general manager of Burroughs Corporation, Saul Kuchinsky. Saul, his daughter and son-in-law, would enroll in Sherborne's first course.

This stateside visit afforded an opportunity to meet with people who were interested in Bennett's other line of work. A mix of Eastern collegiate—as he put it, "hippie" types—showed a passion for work ideas and assured him that a year's stay in Boston or New York would draw many people.

THIS BRINGS HIS story up to 1970. One final, incongruous curtain-call for the turbulent decade came in the summer of 1969: the Americans stepped onto the Moon. The event aroused the admiration of the world, momentarily reviving

America's pride of accomplishment, as if to herald a new epoch which, as it turned out, did not arrive. Faith in the future was the missing ingredient. Some twenty years hence, I would hear some television comedian capture our numb ambivalence in an icy one-liner: "That's gotta be the biggest thing to hit the scene since what's-his-name walked on the Moon."

The times were not auspicious. A sober pall settled over my own country. America's Boer War in Southeast Asia would not end without someone eating crow. Iconoclism passed for wit; the promise of a world-wide humanitarian embrace, a bad joke.

The mood was similar in Europe as well, I remember. People everywhere were weary of the cartoon idiocy of geopolitical posturing, especially between America and the Soviet Union. Europe and America had sustained, for better or worse, a wide-spread psychic shake-up: LSD, courtesy of Sandoz laboratories and the Alpert and Leary experiments at Harvard.

These events were not lost on Bennett. He took great interest in the pop festival phenomenon and attended the famous Glastonbury concert, among others. He witnessed in these gatherings a new emerging social arrangement, having the capacity for attracting and participating with higher energies.

When Bennett saw the enthusiasm of the young Americans he met, he returned to England with mixed feelings about his future role as entrepreneur or as retired author. Times had changed and were full of potential.

A convert to Catholicism in later years, Bennett retired for a short spell to St. Wandrille, a Benedictine Monastery in France to which he had access, and entered into the regimen of prayer and meditation in order to come to a decision. Neither course was chosen, as he records in *Witness,* but he received instead an injunction to start a school. "I thought it referred to the education project, but it quickly became clear that I was called to an entirely new undertaking."

Why a school, what kind, and for what purpose, had to be asked and understood. Bennett must have considered the prospect of an academy for continuous education over a long period of time, in spite of his getting a sudden message from above. His first year was highly organized and well thought out, considering what he would attempt to do. But a resurgent interest in work ideas had unexpectedly appeared among young people. This in itself suggested that the school must function on those principles and techniques, but for what purpose?—since the fabled Fourth Way school only exists to serve some purpose outside itself. (Not a bad formula for any enterprise, when you think about it.) The alienation from existing institutions, traditions, and forms of belief indicated a need for new ideas: people must be prepared for the troubles ahead.

He returned to England and announced the plan. On the questions of money, a place for housing such an enterprise, and people willing to give up a year of their lives to uninterrupted involvement, all of which were presently lacking, his position was simple: if the injunction was authentic, the means would be provided.

CHAPTER ~ FOUR

IN LATE AUGUST, 1971, the repose of Sherborne village was disturbed by the daily arrival of strangers, mostly young, long-haired Americans and Londoners, who were setting up housekeeping in Lord Sherborne's vacant manor house. The high walls of the estate provided a terminus to the main street, with its one general store and village "club". (The Dutton family, who had owned everything in the village for centuries, forbad the traditional pub, but allowed for a licensed bar.) The villagers were accustomed to the occasional tourist—this was the heart of the Cotswolds, after all, and Sherborne House had previously been a school for 140 boys. There were rumors that this late enterprise came to an inauspicious end: The entire student body had mutinied and ran riot through the house—inspiring an exaggerated film version which was released in England the previous year.

Within the building was evidence of willful destruction, walls punched with gaping holes and so on, especially in some of the large state rooms which had served as dorms.

Sherborne House lay a mile off the A-40 highway between Oxford and Cheltenham, about eighty miles west of London. Lord Charles Sherborne, like many of his class, had been obliged to liquidate the family estate, which modern times had transformed into a costly anachronism after some years of abandonment. Mrs. Elizabeth Bennett found it was available, describing it by telephone to her husband, still on his lecture tour in America. The house and grounds, minus the stable block, went for 30,000 pounds. The estate included fifteen acres of gardens, paddocks and outbuildings, on which the 60,000 square foot house stood in Georgian repose. Early records show charter to the monks of Winchcombe Abbey a monastic grange, in 1182 AD. The monks, it seems, settled the land as early as 811 AD, when a small chapel was constructed within the footprint of the present-day edifice The oldest pre-existing structures are at the rear of the house. The stone floor of the kitchen contained a sole remnant of the first monastery: An incongruous window opening, where Winchcombe monks had received their rations of bread.

The house was skewed about a central courtyard, with restrained, dignified limestone facades composed of ample, straight-headed bay windows and perpendicular detailing. The edifice was constructed so close to the parish church that they appeared to be connected. The front entrance, a deceptive understatement of three steps up to the vestibule, led into a great hall, a hundred feet in length, all laid in Cotswold stone. Two tiers of steps, shrouded in shadow, led to a grand staircase leading up to the second-floor ballroom, the dining room, the largest of the house's two libraries, and spacious drawing rooms, all illuminated through tall mullioned windows.

The enormous house was all but deserted when Sally and I arrived, accompanied by Michael Sutton. "Mick," a nickname he went by more often than not in his homeland, had been told that two or three people would be found on the property. I unloaded our luggage and paid the driver, who was gaping incredulously at the massive stone regalia above him, perforated across its length in broken panes and boarded windows. "Good luck," was his parting shot as he wheeled the taxi around for the journey back to London.

Mick, his one suitcase in hand, tried the front door, which opened onto a large entrance hall. From there we set off slowly through the dark warrens of the house, looking for signs of life. Someone heard our hellos, and directed us to seek a young Englishman out back who would help us get settled. We found Tim some distance from the house, hanging washing on a line above the crannied ruin of a tennis court. By evening we somehow made a meal for ourselves without benefit of a stove or electricity. We spread our bedding onto the bare wood floor of one of the great, echoing rooms, within the nimbus of a single candle wedged into the neck of a bottle.

People showed up, singly, in pairs, in families, over the following days and weeks to join in a big renovation effort before the official opening. Gaping holes in the plaster, peeling wallpaper, extensive water damage, broken windows, and the normal results of prolonged neglect could be seen everywhere. The roof needed sealing and flashing along its many parapets, chimneys, and ridges, a job performed at a dizzying height along steep, slick metal roofing. The electrical wiring was brittle and dangerously exposed in many places. Much of it had to be replaced and new circuits and power panels installed. The central hot water supply repeatedly broke down, as the antiquated boiler and piping needed a complete refurbishing. Typical of these large English houses, the private rooms relied on fireplaces to take off the chill. The many rooms not oriented toward direct sunlight, particularly those that looked out into the central courtyard, were permeated with a dampness that would conduct the coming winter chill down to the bone.

The kitchen itself was a cavernous room on the ground floor, with high windows open to the inner court. Against the opposite wall was a row of Agas—massive, built-in coal-fired ovens which could be damped for roasting and baking while simmering food or bringing cauldrons of water to a boil on their armor plate cooktops. The system of flues and fireboxes needed a thorough cleaning, which took from Mick Sutton many days of backbreaking labor and continuous cleanup. The Hobart, a powerful machine for mixing bread dough, was purchased and installed. Meanwhile, as more and more students arrived to join the work crews, meals had to be prepared on a used electric range, hastily purchased for a few pounds. Hot water for the scullery crews had to be heated by the same means.

It was impossible to say at what point the group of strangers became a functioning community. The process seemed to have begun before the first arrival. The general state of disrepair and lack of amenities were made bearable by the evidence of steady improvement and by Bennett's confident presence, which somehow infused the house with a sense of order. He looked quite at home in the role of landed gentry: broad-rail corduroys, woolen necktie under a heavy cardigan, the long, beaming face and eyes which took in the whole surrounding. His seventy-odd years vested him with a reassuring presence. Despite the apparent absurdity of the conditions, everything was just as it ought to be. Elizabeth's patience steadied the place; she was accustomed to an environment of frequent crisis.

Bennett saw to it that the course (the ten month training program was referred to as the "basic course") effectively commenced as soon as the early volunteers arrived. We arose for "morning exercise" (a sitting practice similar to active meditation) in the Great Hall and broke in the afternoon for movements. After the evening meal, he read to us from Gurdjieff's book, *Beelzebub's Tales to His Grandson,* or just talked to us for the hour. In every other way he remained unobtrusive, and the conditions of the house evolved with a minimum of instruction. As more of us arrived, the frenetic energies that people generate among themselves increased but were contained. No rules were set down, except for a restriction against the use of drugs, but clearly it was expected that we try to be present in whatever we were doing. This in itself created an atmosphere that new arrivals could immediately sense and adopt without much explanation.

One of Bennett's staff, Gilbert Edwards, was a precise man with a no-nonsense manner, charged with getting the physical conditions into order and making the best use of the available help. He quickly recognized people with managerial abilities and put them in charge of various teams. He hovered over the activity of the house like a specter, which drew from people a greater attention to detail and probably a significant reduction in accidents. As I remember, no one sustained a serious injury during this period. There were close calls however: One student has for a memento, a blued knife blade with a half-moon of blade missing. He cut through what was mistaken for a dead circuit. From sheer luck, or something more providential, he was unharmed.

A similar close call happened to me one morning, when I was assigned to help the local electricians in rewiring the mansion. They debated the wisdom of cutting through what both of them concluded were dead lines. The electrician who seemed to be in charge was sure the wires were dead, but for good measure he advised me always to stand on non-insulating material, "such as that box right there," he said, pointing to the wood crate conveniently located next to me. Purely a matter of sensible precaution. Then his assistant remembered a point along the circuit where they might double check. The head electrician said there was no need since he knew all the lines passing through the room were dead. There was a slight pause, a split-second ripple of uncertainty, before they turned and left. I proceeded, dumbly resigned to this semi-conscious piece of consensus-building. Having finished cutting through the old, brittle wires tucked high in the joist space, I heard two pair of feet cantering down the flagstones. The electrician saw the cut wires and said, with a laugh, "Well, I guess they were dead ..." They had discovered an untraced high voltage feed. If it were the one I cut through, it could have killed me. Some might say that the house was protected. In my case I think it was sheer luck.

The work crews put in twelve-hour days, painting or prepping walls, ceilings, door and window casings, trying to stay at least one room ahead of the painting crews. Damaged walls were re-lathed and plastered; sections of tongue-in-groove flooring were replaced. The grandest state rooms, with high, corniced ceilings and intricate bay windows, took days to refinish. There were forty-four bedrooms and state rooms in all, several of which served as dorms, private rooms for whole families, and double rooms. The smallest rooms on the third floor were reserved for couples, or those who paid extra for private quarters. Furniture was purchased and sparingly apportioned to the various rooms, and we established ourselves in our assigned spaces as soon as the paint had dried. The rhythm of life at Sherborne began to take shape.

As the commencement date approached, the candidates arrived each day in greater numbers. In spite of the preponderance of young adults, most of whom bore a signature of the counterculture in dress, personal grooming, or demeanor, there was an unexpected variety of humanity filling out the ranks.

A close-knit family of Quakers crammed themselves into the double rooms over the kitchen, nearest the chapel. The mother, Anja Liengaard, daughter of a knighted architect, preferred dressing like a country peasant and wearing her black and gray hair in a single braid down her back. She and her husband, Keld, were among Bennett's former students. They had leased their English farm for the year and brought their four children with them. Everyone in the family played a different instrument and occasionally gave a concert of Welsh, Cornish, and other folk music. Keld was a Danish farmer, who would provide most of the expertise in animal care and gardening methods, as well as set up an arts program. It would be he alone who would rise in the night to assist in the birthing of the new lambs.

A family of Mormons came from Arizona. Virgil Walker was an ex-law enforcement officer with an undisguised distaste for the hippie community, now complicated by the prospect of being surrounded by them every day for the next ten months. Physically he fit the part, with his jet black mustache and slow and deliberate speech. He would go through a visible transformation before the year was out. They arrived with a Scot and his American wife. The incongruity of the group was partly explained by the fact that both men had studied under the same professor of philosophy, by the name of Goyette, a remarkable teacher who had kindled in them an interest in work ideas, subsequently leading them to Bennett.

George and Mary Cornelius came from Alaska. George presented himself as a die-hard Republican and a Nixon loyalist, whose disapproval of hippies was equal to Virgil's but more vocal. A man of contradictions, he brought a half-dozen of his own students from Alaska, the long-haired variety. His wife was an elfin woman of perfect kindness and a patient composure that counterbalanced George's natural surliness.

Other families and single mothers arrived, among them some veterans of Coombe Springs days. Together with the Bennetts' two younger daughters, there were some fifteen children, from toddlers to early teenagers. The house was a vast, evocative stage for their games, and their excited shouts and laughter echoed down the long hallways and came in through the windows from the lawns and gardens.

A quiet English gentleman in his eighties, by the name of Richard Duffell, enrolled and unfailingly participated in all the activities, including Movements and garden work, in spite of a body that had all the typical infirmities of advanced age. I asked where he got the dollar-sized indentation at the temple region of his skull. From a bullet in World War I. An American woman in her sixties, Avis Paxton, en route to Sherborne, caught the attention of the young woman seated next to her on the flight to London. Lynn O'Brien came for a visit out of curiosity and found herself asking to be admitted to the program. Bennett accepted her, after which enrollment was closed.

Behind the house, in a large, unheated outbuilding converted into a studio, lived the painter Gerald Wilde, whose paintings hung in London's Tate Gallery. He is known in art and literary circles as the model for Gulley Jimson, the eccentric artist-hero of Joyce Cary's *The Horse's Mouth,* one of Alec Guinness's more memorable incarnations. Gerald had lived through years of suffering and isolation, a complete antithesis to the inner freedom Cary's fictional hero was meant to personify. He had somehow come into contact with the Bennetts, who gave him lodging first at Coombe Springs, now Sherborne, seeing that he was safely provided with the materials to continue his painting. Bennett regarded Gerald as a rare genius. Gerald was creating a series of paintings whose details sometimes became dustjacket designs for Bennett's and Tony Blake's publications. He tried valiantly to take meals with the rest of us, but the rituals of social intercourse drove him back to unbroken privacy. We took turns bringing his meals.

Gerald's conversation was never projected at you; he might just as well be addressing an invisible presence. His remarks seemed disjointed, until one became oriented to his bewildering use of unclarified pronouns and finally understood that by "he" Gerald invariably was referring to Mr. Bennett. Gerald said Mr. Bennett was a magician. In Gerald's case, he was—having wrested Gerald from a ten-year shut-in of unremitting despair: mainly, looking at the image of himself in a mirror until someone brought the Bennetts into his life.

Once, Gerald was standing behind me while I looked at a photo—pinned up in his stableblock room—of a Greco-Tartar looking dervish (Gurdjieff himself) in white robes and the conic Mevlevi hat. I asked, "You mean him?" "No, not him. Mr. B.," Gerald explained. Then he looked at Gurdjieff's photograph and said jokingly, "He would have scared me to death!" and passed me a tea biscuit.

A few of us earned his trust and found him to be a compassionate man with an utterly original mind. Others found him unpleasantly disorienting and avoided him altogether.

Many of the American students had come to Sherborne through contact with other group leaders—Robert de Ropp, Irmis Popoff, Paul and Naomi Anderson, Alex Horne, Mary and George Cornelius. For these students, Sherborne appeared to be established in the spirit of Gurdjieff's Prieuré, which the director was forced to close due to a severe automobile accident. Sherborne would be blessed with uninterrupted time and seclusion for the purpose of practice. Most of the practical techniques, hidden away since Gurdjieff's death, would be assembled in one place, with the intention of accelerating the process of their assimilation.

A few came from their own unique directions: A mathematician who had immersed himself in *The Dramatic Universe;* a psychotherapist who had put his Bay Area practice on hold for the year; two students of Sufism, enjoined by their teacher to go to Bennett whom they regarded as part of their tradition.

My friend Eric Davis, with his wife Ann, arrived a week or two after me. Eric was a large man, bearing a physical and facial likeness to the American storyteller, Garrison Keillor. He had a strong stutter, which gave him compensatory time to think far ahead of most of his listeners. His devious sense of timing gave his jokes and stories high marks for style and his pronouncements a special weight. Although we grew up as contemporaries from the same town, we only encountered each other at a summer camp and, later, in high school. Eric initiated me into good science-fiction. His taste at thirteen was precocious and discerning. He became a kind of mentor, to whom I sometimes unburdened my teen-age anxieties. Eric brought a reserved, critical eye to the proceedings. He was incapable of taking things on authority. But Bennett's insistence early on to verify everything by personal experience must have reassured him.

Of a reasonable and earthly intelligence, Eric also had a rather incongruous gift for premonition, an instance of which involved my return from India. He foresaw that I would be bringing back something of great importance to him. This seemed unlikely, as we had not seen each other for years. He was attending college in Knoxville. But Ann nodded her head emphatically, confirming this revelation, just after I told him about the school in England I wanted to attend.

The Academy was meant to be international, in fact was seeking affiliation with the World University under United Nations auspices. Apart from the English and Americans, international representation for the first course was provided by a Brazilian, a Norwegian, a Swiss-German and a Scot (both holding U.S. citizenship) an Argentine with English roots, and a Danish farmer, his English wife and their children. Anna Durco, our Movements teacher, was a Slovak from Chicago, multi-lingual from childhood. There were no Asians or Africans. The first test group in the Sherborne experiment would be mainly composed of Jewish and Christian English-speaking Caucasians: fifty-two men, thirty-eight women.

CHAPTER ~ FIVE

THE FIRST OFFICIALLY scheduled event of the Academy, on October 17, 1971, was a kind of inaugural address. Mr. Bennett sat in a wing chair placed in the middle of the ballroom. The bare surfaces of the room amplified the smallest sound as we crept about in our socks, grabbed pillows and found a place to sit. I watched him as he watched us.

This man of unusual height made a small and solitary figure in the empty volume of the room. Rain-sodden light from the windows gave the floor a cheerless sheen. The dimensions of the space seemed out of scale. Or was it we who were out of scale?

The psychological effect of the space enhanced a rising apprehension. I had the uncomfortable feeling of someone discovering he has boarded the wrong train. I looked around at all of us together. How young most of us were!

Those of us who arrived days or weeks before were already on a first-name basis, and relationships had begun to be established; but now I felt we were becoming aware of each other for the first time.

"The first expression of the purpose of this course of study," Bennett began, "is that of freedom—both inner and outer." Inner freedom is attainable by denying our habits, drives, hungers, stimulants, laziness, and so on. Some measure of inner freedom must be attained before we can even attempt to work for outer freedom, which he described as independence from outside impressions and forces, including those generated by other people.

Another way of expressing the aim of the school is to learn how to work, and to work from our own understanding and initiative. This also implies a great deal of inner freedom. He said that most of us already understood that we cannot work like this, but that we haven't grasped why this is so. He said it is because we have no channel to that part which enables us to work from ourselves—the channel to our own conscience.* That brought him to a third and, in his opinion, the best expression of the aim of the course: to help people find conscience and learn to live by conscience rather than by rules, or external morality, or by their feelings and impulses.

* Gurdjieff writes in *Beelzebub's Tales to His Grandson* (Chaps. 27 & 28) that conscience is the only sacred being impulse surviving in relatively undistorted form in man's subconscious (as opposed to faith, hope, and love), and therefore is the last remaining means for man to have a direct connection with the Creator.

"It is a wonderful thing to be able to live by conscience," he warned us, "but very difficult for those accustomed to live under external influences and their own habits and impulses. Though everyone in this room would say they wish to be able to live by conscience, if they could really see what this means, they might decide to take the next train home and not go on with this. There's no external ruler, no external teacher that makes such demands on us as our own conscience. When it is awakened and we have learned to listen to it, it reveals to us what we need to do. Conscience is really the creator of our own individuality."

I understood this. The room suddenly felt cold.

Bennett then spoke of a young man who withdrew his application and left the day before, because he foresaw the hardships that would come and doubted his own endurance. He struck Bennett as having a refined and sensitive nature, with perhaps more promise than most of us who chose to stay. But he was quite right, he said, in following his instincts rather than leaving in the middle of a process to which he was unsuited. I read this as a last opportunity for withdrawing gracefully.

He described three different kinds of work which correspond to the threefold nature of man, the parts of which he called function, being and will. These three lines of work were sequential, creating a natural division of the school's course into three parts. To even speak about will was impossible until some preparation was made in the realms of function and being. But then he qualified this statement with a paradox: "Yet it is perfectly true to say that the three lines of work must be concurrent. Work on function requires a measure of will, or something like it."

He called the three stages of the course the exoteric, or study of our functions; the mesoteric, or work on being; and the esoteric, or work on will.

At this point my mind began to wonder about the meaning of these words, especially his special use of the word *being.* The picture of my graduating from one level of assimilation to another struck me as preposterous. I began to wonder if all of Bennett's lights were on.

To my relief, he was now describing his program in concrete terms. "The starting point of our work," he said, "is in establishing a positive relationship with our own body. Some people have already achieved this to some extent; others may not be accustomed to hard work, have become over-sensitive and squeamish. From these tendencies we would need to free ourselves."

His eyes took us all in. "Some of you are now sitting cross-legged on the floor, a position which is uncomfortable if you are not used to it. It can be so disturbing and occupy so much of your attention that it interferes with everything else. This is because your body is not yet obedient to you."

Several of us straightened our spines and became still. A spirit of resolve entered the room. If there was ever a moment when the course could be said to have begun, this was that moment.

"Next," he continued, "we must come to the emotional work. You are here, a number of people who shall have to live and work together for the next ten months. We shall produce reactions in one another, of like and dislike, of irritation and impatience. We shall see people doing things in a way we think they should not be done; we shall find all these thing hard to bear. This will give us the most effective means of self-liberation: learning to bear the unpleasant manifestations of others. Here we can learn to transform our negative reactions to other people into positive states; to take for ourselves the energy that we should otherwise lose. Unless we are able to work in this way, we won't have the strength to do all the rest of the work that is required."

More so, he added, we must free ourselves from the illusion within us that we count and other people don't, that we are the center of existence. Every day as we work together, opportunities will arise for overcoming this egocentricity. At any moment one may feel irritation, impatience, a wish to complain, a feeling of self-pity, doubts of the good intentions of others. When one sees this kind of emotional impulse arise, one must see this as an opportunity and be thankful that such situations come to us; without them there would be no possibility of attaining freedom.

My apprehension fled. The school was endowed with the raw material of human interaction, which I already knew first-hand thanks to my recent emotional collision with another student. We had shared breakfast duty, which included the preparation of a massive amount of porridge. It was an overnight process which began by bringing many gallons of water to boil in a huge pot, itself a slow process, relying only on the radiant heat of the Aga. An exact amount of steel-cut oats were to be sifted into the water without breaking the rolling boil. After some moments of stirring until it began to thicken, the pot was to be covered and left in one of the Aga's oven compartments to finish cooking at low heat until morning.

About to measure out the oats at the far end of the kitchen, I asked my fellow cook to verify the amount from the recipe file, located at the table where he was working. It developed that the recipes had been removed and could not be readily found; but he found a container of oats, read the label, and multiplied the proportions accordingly. But I had seen the porridge made before, and memory told me the quantity he arrived at could not be correct.

I pictured myself facing one hundred-plus hungry adults and their children filing past, each one holding out their empty bowl, and me in my cook's apron ladling out a meal I had totally botched. I could visualize the speed with which the news would progress to the end of the line, as I spooned out globules of congealed porridge; or, by exceeding an equally narrow margin of error in the opposite direction, a broth as thin as the milk to go with it. I reasserted my doubts, and he indulged me by rereading the formula and recalculating the proportions out loud, which I still could not believe had a chance of being right. I urged that we find someone else who recently made the porridge, but he insisted that it was unnecessary: the proportions sounded right to him on the basis of his own past experience. He had staked his ground.

I had previously observed in this fellow a streak of impulsive self-assertiveness, which I personally found irritating to begin with, and this only served to strengthen my doubt. But just as my own self-will was mobilizing, I realized that I could make a "work effort" out of the situation by putting his judgment before my own. I gave in, with magnanimous good cheer.

Later, after everything else was made ready and the dining room was laid out, we returned to the Aga to check the porridge. It was of such a watery consistency that I was sure something was wrong. He then looked at the label once again and discovered he had all along been misreading the units of measurement, mistaking quarts for gallons or some such thing.

I gave him the silent treatment as we dumped out the useless batch, scrubbed out the pot, stoked the Aga back up and waited another hour for a new potful of water to boil. We finished at around one in the morning, whereby I returned indignantly to my room.

I reacted to the incident for a long time afterwards, and it colored my whole perception of him as a person. But it was not until much later that my own part in the affair dawned on me: I should have searched out the recipe file myself or verified the recipe with someone else, particularly since my instincts were signaling to me so strongly. In short, I had made a decision to follow a course of action and shifted the responsibility for its failure onto someone else.

Bearing the unpleasant manifestations of others is not a born skill. What started out as an effort at practicing selflessness, ended in my becoming self-righteously resentful. My reaction was shallower yet, resulting not so much from the middling inconvenience he caused me, as the fact that I found his manner "irritating."

This incident reminds me of Bennett's oft-repeated warning: most efforts will require another effort, without which our work comes to nothing. Such practical experience in the business of work on oneself was his real contribution to our education.

BENNETT CLOSED his address: "I do not believe that all this would be possible unless we had help. I would not have undertaken this task myself unless I had been convinced that I would be given help in undertaking it, and that you yourselves will benefit from it. We shall be able to work together if we do all that we can ourselves, and if we open ourselves to receive help from the source from which the decision originally came. It is in serving a purpose which is not our own, but which has been given to us, that we find our own reality; but also in serving that purpose we are given the help to accomplish what we otherwise could not possibly do."

The ballroom lost its cheerless emptiness. He had energized it, and us, with his confidence and faith. No list of do's and don'ts, beyond implying a few sensible attitudes for community living, such as not spending five minutes washing a single cup when meals for a hundred must be prepared regularly, whereupon Sherborne was effectively put into our hands. We would operate it. We were its material for study, its curriculum.

As we rose and set the cushions back against the walls, ready to depart for our first scheduled assignments, Bennett announced we would hold future assemblies in the main library, a room more in scale to our number. The floor of the library was covered with broad Asian carpets, very handsome, and surrounded by bookshelves filled with hardbound collections belonging to Bennett personally and to the Institute established at Coombe Springs.

CHAPTER ~ SIX

MUCH OF THE teaching at Sherborne was imparted in the form of talks. I calculate that we participated in six hundred hours of lectures and discussions, where we were fed ideas, theory, and illustrative material. Taking notes was discouraged; if one wished to preserve something while the impression was fresh, it had to be on the run, or before retiring after a long and densely scheduled day. The great majority of these ninety-minute talks were given by Bennett extemporaneously, thrice, as the ninety students were subdivided into three separate groups.

After all those sessions, my recollections consist mostly of internal states, while preparing a meal, spading a garden, reacting to someone's behavior, or watching how well or badly some task was going. Intense or significant moments transpired in the most ordinary of circumstances.

Of the day the course officially commenced, one memory stands out: I was standing before the tackboard outside the dining hall, on which was posted a weekly schedule. I found my name listed under "Group C." I could barely absorb the information; I was suddenly repelled by the similarity with my collegiate past, which seemed to be nothing more than a receding blur of class schedules. Everything I had read about the methodology of the Work prepared me to expect the unexpected. This tidy compartmentalization of time struck me as absurd.

"How English!," I said to myself, "They remembered to schedule tea at four." I had the sinking premonition that the Work was about to be institutionalized, and I had just enrolled in yet another year of academics.

The feeling was most untimely, rising up at the very hour the course was to begin in earnest and filling me with apathy. I felt I was being denied a great fund of energy needed to undertake this psychological work, which was somehow due to me since I had traveled so far, paid the money, and so forth. And then the self-questioning came: Was this sinking feeling the first honest measure of my interest—or lack of it? Had all the book reading, talks with yogis, theosophists, Ouspenskians, Sufis, fellow seekers, travels in Asia, all been a pretense? The quest for self-knowledge suddenly lost its sparkle: I could not find anything inside me that seriously wished to struggle, to work. My untimely lack of enthusiasm was like a mask dropping. I felt vaguely sick, staring dumbly at Group C's schedule of work periods:

6:30 AM	Bell
6:45 AM	Morning Exercise
7:30 AM	Breakfast
9:00 AM	Gardening

Some incubus had crept in and stolen my will. I could not but look hard and long at everything that brought me here. Reasons could not be found, only images borrowed from other people's lives—images of the young man in search of a biography or some great cause to build a life around. Or, perhaps, a need for a father figure, a wise elder like Bennett, who at least looked the part.

I stood there in the hallway for quite some time, brooding on my life. Whenever I looked within to find a self, I found there was nobody home. I needed to be told when still an adolescent, but never was, that it is not abnormal to perceive other people as real, while finding oneself unreal. I beheld people by their outer shell, as full-blown beings, with names and histories, allotted characteristics and abilities. I interacted with the world largely by impersonation of whatever I thought might make a favorable impression on people, or at least hide my littleness from them. Everyone around me seemed to be harboring a secret about life they forgot to let me in on. Against all evidence of my own even rather varied experience, I still unconsciously perceived other people as wholes. I coveted their knowledge and abilities. My insubstantiality was a material problem: knowing nothing, unable to do anything, I was nothing. Worse yet, I had not been able to force myself to learn anything useful.

I dwelled in my imagination so much in my youth that I earned a reputation for absentmindedness. My environment just did not hold my interest; or, if it did, only as a theater stage with ready-made sets for my daydreams. The one positive value my parents articulated was respect for hard work. That value turned out to be gold. But as for psychological insight, that is, hints about how the world works, I got zero. My parents did not and could not prepare me, but 1950's American culture could and did. It broadcast a message which I interpreted without hope: life consists of finding out what one is good at, and by developing such ability, one eventually becomes somebody. There was a short list of recognizable vocations I could choose from. Being on that list was the sole criteria for occupations that passed as "useful." Poetry, like philosophy, was for dreamers and deadbeats, unless it landed a teaching job. There was one way out—the luck of the draw—to be born to genius or special talent. If one showed signs of neither at an early age, it was best to pick a specialty and become it as soon as possible.

Finding no tendency in myself but for tuning out the world around me, I looked forward with increasing dread at approaching adulthood. Nothing of myself seemed to be growing except my body. If anything, it was this that brought me here. Regardless of the naivete of Bennett's expectations, just remembering that I had a reason for coming revived me.

I recount all this, because it helps illustrate the nature of life at Sherborne.

Our motives for coming were from an inner need to experience conditions resembling that of a pressure cooker. The subject of the course was ourselves. Already at the outset, before anything external had been introduced—a lecture, an idea, or a task—self-assessment was set in motion by virtue of my decision to enroll. I was standing at the bottom of Albert Camus' hollow tree, looking up at the patch of sky above and wanting to climb out, without the energy or knowledge to make a first move. But there was a wish, or else I would not be standing there. Help would have to come, which is precisely where Bennett entered the picture.

10:30 AM	Psychology
12:00 PM	Dinner
1:00 PM	Cosmology
2:30 PM	Movements
4:00 PM	Tea
4:30 PM	Personal Time
5:30 PM	Reading
6:30 PM	Supper
7:30 PM	To be Announced
9:00 PM	Meditation
10:30 PM	Retire

SHERBORNE HOUSE WAS a teaching machine. Aside from a handful of assistants who were responsible for special classes, planning meals, and the purchasing and allocating supplies, everything was performed by the students. This included the cooking of meals, caring for the children, maintaining the house and grounds, planting and harvesting the gardens and so on. Without this, there was little opportunity to apply what was taught. Bennett assured us that if the Academy had unlimited funds, there would be no increase of staff; the essential ingredient for learning would come out of the daily needs of the community. This was accomplished in a straightforward way, by dividing us into three groups of equal size, so that each group could take over the responsibilities of the household every third day, thereby freeing the other two groups for work sessions. Periodically the student body was reshuffled, giving the opportunity for a more complete interaction among all the members.

Whoever was assigned the task of house supervisor would in turn assign each member of the group to their particular task. Usually more than one duty would be assigned, such as: child care in the morning, house maintenance in the afternoon. Cooking and serving meals to the entire household became routine, although many of us were nearly useless in the kitchen when we first arrived. The chief cook would be appointed, under which were assistants, kitchen boy, and scullery crew. Upstairs, serving crews set out the tableware, carried out the meals from the servery, washed up and restored the dining room for the next meal. Each day bread would be made from freshly ground flour, to be served on the following day. Two of the housekeeping crew would come on duty the night before, after the final activities of the evening ended, to prepare for breakfast.

Breakfast cooks were the first to rise the following morning, to stoke the Agas, slice the loaves of bread for toasting, and awake the household at the appointed time. One of them would walk all three floors, ringing a bell that resounded down the long, carpetless corridors. Within a minute people emerged from their rooms on their way to the lavatories to perform "ablutions"—a ritual rinsing of the face, forearms, feet, and genitals with cold tap water, which in the winter could be especially bracing.

Ben Bennett was a twenty-year-old likeness of his father, recalling the much-published photo of the young WWI Captain in his knee-high lace-ups: intelligent, autocratic, supremely self-confident. Ben's own self-confidence became instantly famous throughout the house the morning following his arrival. Men and women came out of their rooms to the common wash rooms and to the tub and shower rooms for ablutions. We had learned to maneuver about the facilities with as much decorum as possible, careful to be appropriately robed, if only in towel, and settled on the lavatory rooms being used by both sexes at the same time. The arrangement was obliterated in an instant as Ben entered, pulled off his towel, claimed one of the double row of lavs, splashed handfuls of water onto his genitals and the rest of his person, and cleared out his nose into the running water, all in about fifteen seconds flat. Quickly brushing his teeth, he replaced his towel around his waist and stalked out.

The women were visibly shocked but recovered and went about their business: the following morning no women showed up in that room, but to its opposite down the hall, where they could complete their toilet without crossing Ben's path. It was a one-man palace revolution. It also expedited the only sensible arrangement, given that all ninety of us must wash, dry, brush and comb in the fifteen minutes between bell to morning exercise. Perhaps Ben knew exactly what he was doing; he certainly acted the part. Perhaps Bennett, seeing how awkwardly we were utilizing the facilities, told him to do it.

WITH THE ENTIRE HOUSE roused to life, the two cooks would continue to prepare the breakfast while everyone assembled in the ballroom. During this, the morning exercise, the house returned to stillness while the cooks laid out butter, honey, milk, pitchers of water, and brewed the tea and coffee.

The ballroom was cavernous in the pre-dawn. A low fire in the hearth cast a dim glow on the hardwood floor as women and men divided and took their places on opposite sides of the room. Everyone sat cross-legged on mats, cushions, or on the floor itself. Bennett took his seat at one end and directed us through inner exercises that demanded a great deal of sustained attention.

As the weeks progressed, new exercises were introduced, each of them requiring skills developed by previous exercises. It became evident that they formed a graduated series, beginning at an elementary level, where one learned first to distinguish between attention and thought. If anything was common to all the work at Sherborne, it was the directing of attention without which none of what followed would have been possible.

This is a completely different affair from one's attention being engaged by an outside stimulus or by a random thought or feeling. The act of directing one's attention produces the momentary but unmistakable impression of being in charge. My ability to maintain the effort continuously was small; but the length and breadth of our attention can change by the practice of directing it, just as the body changes through exercise. Beginning the day with this collective effort put everything in a certain perspective, where the very presence of other members of the community was, at least potentially, a reminding factor for reviving my lapsing awareness.

When the session in the ballroom was over, I would rise and walk in measured strides, as if transporting a vessel filled to the brim with liquid that could spill over. This precarious balance might last for minutes or be lost before I reached the hallway, so fragile is the hold of our attention, particularly when we are going to a meal.

The dining room was splendidly lit by a bank of high windows looking out over an acre of lawn flanked by formal gardens and hedges, beyond which a clearing surrounded by an old wood rose up to the south. The room itself was elegantly paneled with a Salvine ceiling and capacious sideboard with ornamental cabinet faces. At breakfast, we lined up to receive bowls of porridge and toast handed out from the servery. At dinner and supper, servers appointed from the housekeeping group would bring plates of food to each of us, as we waited.

This produced an interesting and dynamic situation. The role of food in our lives was vividly exposed. The habit of overeating is relative to the individual, of course, as is the particular ability to manifest composure while feeling hunger. I confine my comments to my own experience, which was rich enough in material. I recall times when a towering indignation came over me for having been served a portion which was visibly smaller than the "average serving," which I had already assessed with a hawk-like interest. A server could earn my unbounded enmity for depriving me of my fair share. Second servings were available as long as they lasted, which spurred me to pace my eating accordingly.

It is said in the Work, you are where your attention is; and this was seldom clearer to me than when in the dining room. In keeping with Fourth Way work, life at Sherborne had few restrictions on behavior, but one understood that a new attitude toward the eating of food was essential for our aim. In fact, the role of food is more profound than we can know, and the special study we devoted to it showed that everything in our experience was directly related. At some point early on, Bennett introduced the exercise of consciously taking in the first bite of food. This in itself may sound like a small effort; in practice it was extremely difficult to do it with any consistency at all. I recall many times when I sat waiting for the food to arrive, intending to take the first bite with undivided attention, only to discover after half the meal was gone that I had completely forgotten it—probably at the instant when the food was set down before me. The lure of food is powerful. Even before one begins to eat, a series of physiological mechanisms are set in motion, and one's attention is swallowed up whole by the anticipation of the experience.

Throughout the year we fasted periodically. Many of us looked forward to these days with reluctance—as to a period of time marked by deprivation, or a tedious trek through a barren desert. I began to see how, in ordinary life, eating is a form of entertainment, a reward we have come to expect which, when withheld, makes life cheerless and without interest. Fasting in winter is particularly onerous, as the internal body temperature is sensibly lower, and one is beset with drowsiness. Often it was a struggle to resist climbing into the warmth of the bed, fully clothed, and go to sleep. The added attraction to this recourse was awakening nearer to the moment when the fast would end. Even then, a final effort of self-denial was required. The effects of a fast are potentially beneficial, but are easily negated if it is not broken gradually. Gorging oneself after a fast is poison to the system, undoing any of the potential benefit. I soon discovered, however, that following the rule of breaking the fast with a small quantity of light food was followed by a sensation of well-being that could be completely joyous.

Many Americans came with definite ideas of food and diet. Next to the Vietnam War, nothing in society had been more roundly condemned than the pollution of the environment and the horrors of modern food production. People were profoundly disturbed by the excessive use of pesticides and chemicals to increase production and shelf life, achieve uniformity of appearance, and so on. Our generation was convinced that a morass of corrupt economic priorities had altered the means of food production and distribution, with the result that modern society was ignorant of the most rudimentary principles of cooking and eating. Food needed to be organic and unadulterated, prepared in ways that preserved the vital content, ad infinitum. Many had experimented with new diets, based on one or two principal ideas that promised to restore body and mind. The subject of food was an emotional issue, fueled by the current, tacit belief that everything in modern culture was corrupt and needed to be reformed. All this was part of the baggage we brought to Sherborne.

Sherborne meals did not conform to our baggage. Menus were established under the direction of the Bennetts and Lili Helstenius, who was in charge of restocking the supplies within a restricted budget. The rather plain and uncomplicated fare was high in carbohydrates and starches and generally an affront to the new nutritional wisdom. Meat and animal products were consistently used, although in modest proportions, and a version of each course was specially prepared for those who followed a vegetarian diet. Apart from that concession, no new, esoteric nutritional system was followed. If anything, Management had gone out of its way to preserve all the culinary sins of the modern age, with an apparently willful disregard for the needs of the elite, and vulnerable, human machine. Some students threatened to cook their own meals, rather than submit to this bodily pollution.

Bennett dealt with the issue very early into the course. "Your attitudes towards food are self-centered and quite wrong. You are solely concerned with your diet, your health, with vitamins and non-vitamins and so on. This is really a very egoistic attitude towards food. All food is good, and all food can be assimilated by man, providing he himself is in the right state. Your egotism cuts you off from food: you are thinking of yourself, not the food you eat. If you eat food with the right inner state, all food is nourishing and good, and you will need very little food."

This got our attention, though it was initially met with some resistance, which generated further discussion throughout the year. But people soon adjusted to this unorthodox, yet sensible, attitude. Eventually there were less observant vegetarians. A second-year student, Larry, held out through to the end as the lone vegetarian of his course. His status was perilous. Mick Sutton, who supervised the kitchen operation, took great pleasure in making light of people's diets. One day as chief cook he had forgotten to prepare a vegetarian plate for Larry, who just happened to be on the kitchen crew. To the amusement of those able to appreciate Sutton's humor, he chased Larry raucously down the hallways wielding a large kitchen knife and vowing to serve him up to the meat eaters on feast night.

Mick was a superb cook, but not everyone at Sherborne would necessarily know it. He delighted in putting difficulties in the way of the chief cooks, particularly if they were taking pride in their culinary achievement. My future wife, who would attend the fifth course, was the brunt of one of his antics. Given few ingredients to work with, she undertook to make a flavorful gravy to dress up an otherwise austere meal. After carefully nurturing the sauce all morning to an appetizing golden brown, Mick appeared in the kitchen at the last minute and looked over her shoulder. "Beets." he suggested. Betty was horrified but before she could protest, Mick was already returning from the larder and plunked a whole beet into the pot. In no time at all, the gravy turned from gold to a cadaverous gray, after which the lunch bell rang.

FOLLOWING BREAKFAST and after a short interval of free time, the students pulled on Wellingtons, the Englishman's goloshes, and went to various tasks in the gardens and grounds. An enormous amount of untended vegetation had overrun the flower beds. The kitchen garden at the rear of the house, enclosed by high masonry walls, had become an acre of man-high nettles and weeds. Everything was in need of pruning. The first weeks were an intense effort at clearing the kitchen garden for planting, pruning trees, and reshaping the enormous hedges. A field was spaded and planted with sprouting potatoes.

Bennett was of the opinion that all the other scheduled activities of the course, especially all the talking and lecturing, could be eliminated, with the sole exception of gardening and the Movements, and nothing would be lost. This I took to be a calculated overstatement: many of us had soon fallen into a habit of showing up late, sometimes not at all. The experience of working with the soil to many of us was of lesser value than, say, listening to Bennett expound on the role of food in the reciprocal maintenance of the Creation. The garden was where we could see all this happening, but this somehow did not touch all of us with the same authority we accorded to the rest of the day's activities. The sheer practicality of planting and raising our own food might have provoked from Bennett this fantastic claim, that the whole content of the course could be distilled and transmitted through the experience of digging, weeding, planting and maintaining the grounds. We urban dwellers nodded in agreement, but frequently showed up in our own good time to these outdoor work assignments.

No other scheduled activity besides the gardening session was regarded so casually. It would have been unthinkable to come late and disturb, for example, a Movements class. Although gardening was thus exalted by Bennett, the lackadaisical attendance did not noticeably turn around during the course because no rules were enforced. I have an uncertain impression that we became more constant and punctual in the latter part of the year.

Bennett was very serious about his claim, however. He spent much time speaking with us about the different "essence classes" of the natural order. Enormous forces worked relentlessly over the ages in preparing for the appearance of soil in the world. We have trouble visualizing this astonishing substance: a dynamic, germinal structure teeming with biochemical activity; a shapeless, yet highly organized medium which hosts and is transformed by innumerable denizens of the plant, invertebrate, and micro-organic worlds. The thin, sensitive membrane of the planet we call life, in which the planetary and surplanetary energies are absorbed, transformed and exchanged, all begins in the germinal essence of the soil. Bennett's descriptions of the soil and its significance fired our imagination; but he insisted that only by getting one's own hands into the soil and assisting it to bring forth life can one understand any of this.

As soon as Sherborne House was inhabited, a number of sheep of the local variety were purchased which would later furnish us with wool for weaving. The chicken house was repaired and new hens brought in. The enormous volume of nettles were rooted out in surprisingly little time and planting began, rather hastily as it turned out. The first planting of vegetables was promptly eaten by the local rabbits and pigeons, and everything had to be re-sown with more forethought. A team of ninety people proved to be an unwieldy force, not easily directed and controlled. Within a few hours, a group this size can accomplish an enormous amount of work, for good or ill, with the results outpacing the means to manage them.

A large section was set aside for students to plant and maintain their own plots. Bennett got together a team of volunteers to create a circular rose garden, sixty-odd feet in diameter, situated between the dining hall windows and the yew hedge by the orangery. The nine points of the circle were interconnected by narrow lanes of grass, creating plots of different shapes to be planted in various colors, in the pattern of an enneagram.

The orangery was a glazed conservatory which echoed the style of the main house. Numerous flats of sprouting seedlings were set about on long tables. The orangery somehow doubled as an art studio, with a potter's wheel and a bit of clear working space to one side. Facing the orangery was a large swimming pool, exposed to the weather and in need of structural repair. The heat and filtration system had rusted from disuse.

Everywhere one looked, there were grounds, gardens and foliage to be tended, walls and footpaths to be repaired, lawns to be maintained, animals to be fed and cared for. As the community was to take the active role in maintaining itself and its environment, each member had to begin acquiring necessary skills almost immediately. Garden tools were returned to the tool room only after they were washed clean of corrosive soil; the habit was soon instilled in everyone and enforcement was no longer required. Classes in the care and use of handtools convened in the workshop. A principal feature of the course was exposing us to all kinds of work, to acquire a generalist's ability to learn new skills, including those completely outside one's inclination or interest. Apart from the advantage to a community, where every member is able to perform all essential tasks, an effective means was created for us to observe our functional side by repeatedly putting before us new and unfamiliar activities.

Bennett introduced the first weekly theme, which he called awareness of inanimate objects. No subject could have been more timely, in view of putting the operation and maintenance of an English manor into the hands of a hundred strangers of limited experience. Wrong use of tools results in breakage, waste, and disorder. The task of paying attention to the material object before us, of asking ourselves what this object is for, what its needs are in order to perform its function, how we ourselves make use of the object, and so on, seemed to consolidate us as a group, with its own tenuous, burgeoning level of group awareness. The operation of house and grounds passed into the hands of the students without formality or transition.

During the theme discussion at the end of the week, many of us reported experiences while observing—for instance, how one applied physical force while digging, gauging the optimum leverage of the fork or spade and the stress limit of their wooden handles, and so on—of entering into an unfamiliar new world that had always been before us. In this world, when they are consciously perceived and used according to the purpose they serve, inanimate objects seem to become more fully realized, more fully themselves. "We want to exist," Bennett said, "on higher levels, which we imagine are above the material world. Yet we ourselves exist in a less substantial and lower level than this material plane. The material world is always with us, but we are very seldom in contact with it, even when we have the intention of doing so. We live in dreams, dreaming of higher levels of existence, disdaining what we imagine to be the lowest level, this material world.

In reality, our lives are spent in a level far lower. We rise up to the material level, not down to it."

I said that my most notable experiences usually occurred in circumstances which were outwardly unremarkable. The first theme, on awareness of material objects, revealed the uniqueness of our situation: the enclosed, rural environment, with all its material needs, had become a laboratory in which theory was tested by concrete experience. No separation lay between the classroom and the outside world: study, work, and play was not compartmentalized. We had signed on for a year-long voyage in an enclosed and self-sustaining vessel that exhibited all the features and needs of ordinary life. Our first taste of being the crew of the ship, with the responsibility for keeping it afloat, convinced us that the arrangement was not one of convenience and economy, but the course itself.

AS THE GARDENING SESSION commenced, the housekeeping group turned to their assigned tasks. Breakfast was cleared and the dining room restored. Bathrooms and toilet rooms were scrubbed and cleansed, corridors swept, carpets vacuumed, banisters and casework dusted. A duty which was scrupulously rotated, so that everyone had a turn, was that of house supervisor, who assigned members of the group to the daily tasks and to particular projects he deemed necessary. This responsibility was unique in that the appointed person had to be aware of the entire household and all its functions, the needs of the crew members, the availability of supplies, the scheduled activities, community safety, and so on. The house supervisor was the brain center of the community, the clearing house for information, who handled the details of the day not requiring John or Elizabeth's intervention. The role produced a new mode of awareness: of managing from the top down. House supervisors and chief cooks typically brought some of the most meaningful observations to theme discussions at the end of each week.

Every morning Elizabeth Bennett held practical work sessions for the housekeeping team. Questions put to her were often trivial, if not mindless, the kind that one could ask oneself and then answer with no one's help: should the bathtub be rinsed twice after scouring, and so on. Bennett hinted that we had not learned to make use of Elizabeth. Like Bennett, she was able to make much of a lame question. She helpfully pointed out the typical emotional disruptions, like those occurring when being interrupted in the middle of an activity and being made to turn our attention to something else. This is a time where sensation can save you, she said. Her morning sessions set the tone for house duty as the opportunity for sustained practice.

Elizabeth was a great source of help to me. My way of framing questions is often convoluted, sending the listener off in a different direction from where I am heading. She understood this form of mental disarray and dealt with it productively. She simply stopped me and asked me to begin again, so that she could follow the thread of my question. The direct approach clarified my mind and, subsequently, my speech.

A HOUSEKEEPER WAS assigned to a mid-morning cleaning of the Bennetts' flat, in the wing projecting alongside the village church. A front room offered views in two directions to the facing parkland. A study or parlor, a dining area, and bedrooms which Elizabeth usually kept closed, were painted in an onslaught of primary colors: I remember passing through a field of orange into another of royal blue. Otherwise, the flat was not extraordinary. Sundry items belonging to the two daughters, Hero and Tessa, were scattered throughout. A few small carpets, furniture of varying quality, domestic clutter, Elizabeth's art supplies, a folder of sketches. On a table strewn with correspondence and notebooks, a chessboard was set up with a game in progress. An open newspaper lay next to it, showing the most recent Spassky-Fischer round for world title. From across the room behind me Elizabeth said, "Mr. B. predicts Fischer will mop the floor with him."

Here was Bennett's private world, the one he carried with him from Kingston. Inside the glass-faced bookcase was a leather bound gold-tooled set of *The Dramatic Universe*; some monographs; a few Turkish and Persian titles, including Hasan Sushud's history of the Kwajagan which Bennett was borrowing from for his new book, *Masters of Wisdom*. The rest of his collection, or that of the Institute, filled the house's two libraries. I pulled a book out and found his ex libra inside the front cover: a wood-cut engraving of an ark plying through a storm. A cache of past knowledge, hoping to weather another epoch's dissolution.

In a box of long-playing vinyl records, I found one dating back to the fifties, on the cover of which were two men in conversation. Here was the American producer-entertainer Steve Allen, interviewing a younger Bennett on the then-recent phenomenon of Subud.

We all gained access to the bedroom, when Bennett suffered a hernia early on in the course and was confined to bed for a week or two. He brought each group in and had them find space to sit about the room (by then we were accustomed to sitting on floors) and read to us the latest chapter of another book he was writing.

Elizabeth said more than once, "Mr. B. never wastes a minute. Can you possibly know what that means?" It astonished me that, in the midst of running the school, teaching half the classes and becoming increasingly immersed in private consultation, he could possibly organize his time to write another book. He saw no reason why confinement to bed should halt his active involvement; rather than simply write, he brought everyone in to test the material. After he was back on his feet, it seemed that the rhythm of the course had not experienced so much as a pause.

ONE OF THE most sobering responsibilities everyone shared was child care. Eight young children required supervision while their parents participated in the work sessions. Older children entertained themselves or attended nearby schools. Two housekeepers each were assigned to the morning and afternoon sessions.

For some people, especially the singles and those coming from single-child families, this was a dreadful and often humiliating experience. One felt helpless in front of the disorganized and haphazard condition of the playroom, the lack of clearly defined spaces where activities could proceed without interference, the disarray of the toys and art materials. This lack of order contributed to an immediate and inescapable stress for the children, whose impulses towards possession and utter aversion to sharing created bedlam. People who carried themselves with natural authority, urbane, educated, interesting people with seemingly great promise, suddenly found themselves without inner resources. Child care was the great leveler, where you discovered your limits early on.

The mothers, of course, were greatly concerned about the inadequacies of the children's playroom, and the children's need for outdoor activities. People on child care shared these concerns, but more or less forgot them as soon as the day was over, only to find the conditions little improved when the duty came to them again. One had to devise means to diffuse conflicts, divert the disruptive child, experiment with ways for keeping the children occupied constructively, or at least without damaging anything. This could be excruciating; one might seek inspiration within and find nothing.

The impulse to ignore the situation was always there. I shared child care with an Englishwoman who had been one of Bennett's students for years. Throughout the children's afternoon nap she paced, joking about her unconcealed anxiety for the moment when the little creatures would awake. As the moment closed in, her anxiety was complete; she declared it was all up to me, found a corner to lay down and actually attempted to fall asleep. I related to this; my own state was different only in degree. Somehow I managed to keep things from getting out of hand, but left the session with a disturbing sense of defeat. I saw a cross-section of existence that is usually known only to parents.

The needs of children were sometimes revealed to us in spite of ourselves. Betty Hartzog, a fifth-year student, describes her Sherborne child care experience as follows:

"It was a rainy day. About a dozen children, two to eight years of age, were gathered after breakfast in a damp, mid-sized room. The windows and ceiling of the room were high, so that the shrill voices bounced off of the great masses of hard surfaces. The children had the chaotic and frenzied energy of a damp, winter day.

"I had little experience of being with children. I attempted to calm them with firm supervision, based on safety and civility. At the end of a morning that seemed to go on forever, I felt exhausted and depressed. I had maintained little inner reserve, and any accumulated energy was drained. Surely these poor, cooped-up children deserved better.

"The second time I was given a child care assignment it was again a rainy day. I resolved that this time I would do it differently. Rather than being the authority in charge, I would allow more freedom and stay more open. Playing along with the children, I allowed myself to be the tied-up captive in a game of cowboys and Indians. As time passed, my polite requests to be freed were ignored until I felt desperate. Only anger returned me to a position of authority, which I had hoped to avoid.

"By the third child care session, I had given up and just hoped to get through it. I planned to put my name on a growing list of people who had withdrawn themselves from child care duty. The day was overcast, but we were able to go out of doors. The majority of the children were otherwise engaged, and I was left with two children, a boy and a girl who were both three years of age. Each had a tricycle and we carried out several toys to a stone patio. I mended a teddy bear while the children played.

"Soon the children began to bicker over the same toy, as was their usual pattern. I tried to resolve the issue based on fairness, but the same argument recurred until at last I simply removed the toy, holding it high over their heads. They stared up in amazement—waiting. I had no idea what to do. Seeing their faces, I knew I must provide something immediately. When I asked myself what they needed, the answer came clearly: movement. They followed me onto the great lawn to play follow-the-leader, beginning with a tumbling session. From there we followed whatever took our fancy, the tiny creatures in the grass, the fences for climbing, the pony locked up in a paddock, needing attention. The children were free."

HOUSEKEEPERS BROKE FROM their tasks to attend a ninety-minute session of the special exercises called "movements."

"Exercise" is a really a misnomer, although movements are performed with the body. Assembled in rows and files, the participants execute gestures, turn in circles, change places, and so on. What remains hidden from the viewer is the experience of the performer, consisting of a surprising variety of insights.

In the first days of the course, the few people who practiced movements at Coombe Springs looked no more confident than we newcomers. Most everyone sought positions in rear rows, where one was less exposed and could copy someone else when one became lost, which happened regularly. The instructor typically demonstrated a series of gestures once, after which we were expected to repeat the pattern, no matter how imperfectly.

After taking our places in rows, arm length from one another, Anna Durco, our instructor, started off by doing nothing but standing in place. Everyone was standing in their own fashion, reflecting attitude, self-image, and a lifetime of habit. She studied us silently for a long moment and then began giving different suggestions for finding our center of balance, for reclaiming our full height by pulling our spine out of our hips, our necks out of our shoulders, and so on. The act of standing became a study in itself. Unlike precision drill where one duplicates a modeled posture, Anna's instruction was more concerned with our awareness of our bodies. By directing us to seek out regions that are typically left out of our habitual awareness, our stance became adjusted, as it were, from the inside out.

The pianist sat before the grand, in a windowed alcove, to our right. Students with piano training were recruited and met privately with Bennett and Anna to learn how to play for the classes. The pianist needed to approach the music with respect to the demand each movement placed on the performer, with the result that much of the technique they had acquired for interpreting a piece of music had to be set aside. Between one exercise and the next, the pianist remained seated, composed, waiting for the instructor's signal.

At last the signal came: a concise, pantomimed clapping of hands to set a slow and leisurely tempo. Following Anna's lead, we marched in place. Immediately I found myself out of balance; the pace was slower than my normal gait, and the added difference of remaining in place was enough to create a subtle disequilibrium. Everyone within my peripheral vision appeared to be doing this simple exercise differently: some sent their legs out as if they were bound in splints; others lifted their legs by their knees; others loped, sauntered, or kicked out with staccato bursts of superfluous energy, arms extending to maintain balance. We attempted to imitate Anna's containment and economy of movement. We worked for some time at this ridiculously simple task, trimming our expenditure of energy, fixing the length of our gait and trying to maintain a state of relaxation. Anna signalled for the pianist to vary the tempo and then the rhythm, while we attempted to keep up with the changes.

My breathing was all out of proportion to the task. My balance was just beginning to improve, when Anna made a quarter turn without breaking step. We all did the same. After eight beats, another quarter turn. We were now facing to the rear, leaving our instructor behind us. Craning my neck to catch her next move felt completely inappropriate, leaving me with the decision to turn or not at the end of eight beats without seeing her next move. I made the quarter-turn, relieved to find she had done the same. Two measures later, we were facing front again; a pattern of movement was imparted to us in the first go-around, without verbal instruction. Clearly we were being acclimated to a style of instruction for executing new activities, with little or no formal explanation and variations without warning.

She stopped us and demonstrated a series of arm gestures, simple ones, in a repeating pattern any child could imitate. We marched again, adding the arm positions. As the arms and legs began to work in concert, my body began to experience a certain enjoyment. This was cut short when she told us to stop again. We all stood in place, waiting. After a long moment, she told us to bring our attention back inside ourselves. We stood there for some time, eventually becoming aware that we were haphazardly standing as we had at the beginning of the class, and began to readjust ourselves. I saw that the act of standing, too, was a position like any other, requiring the same intention that was to be brought to any other position. In Movements there was no "dead air" between one effort and the next.

She called for us to take the first arm position. She told us to sense our arm. This verb, "to sense," had taken on a specific meaning owing to the morning exercises. Sensation was a palpable substance in and about our bodies which, by experiment, responded to the movement of our attention. It was a basic tool for our work with movements. My eyes no longer were the main source of information as to what my arm was doing. Again, the gesture was refined from the inside out, rather than by imitation.

We began again, with the piano, working at deepening the presence we had extended into our arms, our feet, and throughout our bodies. The four straight-arm positions, forward, up, sideways, and down, were simple enough. But when Anna added the left arm, she omitted the down position, introducing a larger pattern of four for the right arm as opposed to a pattern of three for the left.

My body short-circuited, signaling that something new and unfamiliar had to be brought to bear, that attention must divide and focus separately upon each of my flailing arms.

What proceeded from this is not easily described. My mind was attempting to track two moving mental pictures which somehow had to merge. Behind the scenes, a command center was sending instructions to my limbs for duplicating this image. Early attempts were full of error, but out of each repetition a sensorial memory accrued in my arms. Lapses of attention were like the cutting off of oxygen: the instant attention wandered, operations broke down; re-focusing it, resuscitated them again. Of all the numerous actions going on in me, attention was the single element that could be brought under conscious control, that could be construed as an act of will. Behind all this came an occasional flash, as if out of a timeless continuum: the impression of "I".

Fueling my effort was desire. In the midst of emotional exasperation, which movements can generate with impish invention, I saw that my wish could be renewed, in much the same way as attention can be renewed. As the exercise unexpectedly came together, a sudden recognition of the model of man as "three-centered being" startled me. I was pleasantly exhilarated. Insight flooded through me. Everything was momentous. My thoughts, my emotional state, the sensations of my body all came together for an instant, in seamless coordination.

Putting all this into words creates the impression of a serial experience. In reality, these experiences, emotional swings, ruptures and redoubling of efforts, and insights into the mechanics of the physical and psychic sides of our being occurred without order. A movements session was a strong emotional cocktail: intrusions of vanity, of pleasing fantasies that I was cutting a striking figure, looking sexy, and so on, were followed abruptly by deflated self-esteem. I felt the muscles of my face register my every negative reaction, for all the world to see, like a bambi in the headlights.

There was a strong element of humor in all this, when one looked for it. Being caught up by a stray thought or impression usually resulted in missing a cue. While being elated by gaining mastery over the two arm positions and marveling at the profound insight flooding into my mind, I suddenly discovered I was the only person in the group who was still facing front. I had not noticed Anna's signal to add the quarter turn. As if jarred out of a daydream, I lurched to the right, while the sublime balance of mind and body unraveled. In panic I eyed the ranks to find someone to copy, hoping the chosen one would have it right. By the time the first class was over, I had a very good picture of my unconnectedness with my own body, the house wherein I dwelled since birth.

Throughout the year we would work daily at specific movements, exercises, and dances of an increasingly ceremonial character. All of them were demanding, but in unpredictably different ways. Some were devotional, reverent and quieting; others were assertive and warrior-like, tapping great reservoirs of energy in the participants and filling the space around us. They embodied an eloquent, timeless language of gesture that transcended culture and religion, by which metaphysical concepts were symbolically enacted and experienced down to the bones. But as our capacities grew throughout the coming months, the lessons of my first few sessions with movements returned again and again, posing the same challenge, to stretch the limits of conscious participation with physical existence.

TEA AT FOUR was followed by some free time before we reassembled in the lower library. Where Bennett read the next few pages of *Beelzebub's Tales to His Grandson* until the dinner bell rang. Something was always scheduled, or improvised, for the evening: another movements session with all ninety students; or listening to musical performances by the students, recordings of Gurdjieff playing the harmonium, or recordings which Bennett had made during his Near Eastern journeys.

Other evenings were set aside for dramatic improvisation, requiring us to manifest actively before one another. We paired off, one partner mirroring the other's continuous gestures and, at a signal, switched roles. We extemporized conversations while assuming unrelated gestures, and participated in other experiments with body language. These sessions were given by Coombe Springs veterans. It was apparent they had experimented with dramatic technique as a means for demonstrating the psychological ideas. Later on, Bennett brought in an American theater group which studied Gurdjieffian methods—John Allen's "Theater of All Possibilities"—to involve all of us in a non-stop two-week workshop.

The evening sessions eventually became the hour for meditation, but it was several months before Bennett introduced meditation into our program. After the last session, we retired to our rooms or else, bristling with excess energy, headed out for the village pub or to some private room where a party had sprung up on the pretext of someone's birthday. Birthdays occurred with auspicious regularity. But if nothing was happening that evening, one could always walk to Sherborne Village and crowd into its single pub.

In the various gatherings, alcohol was broken out; usually beer, or cider, and gin. Alcohol was not forbidden at Sherborne; it was even used in judicious measure at the Saturday night feasts, where the public could attend. We were left to discern for ourselves our own limits. I do not remember Bennett once mentioning that such activity be restrained, regardless of how noisy things got after hours, at first with pop music and dancing, which lost its appeal soon enough. The music struck us as incongruous, and the dancing consisted mainly of several people simply jumping up and down in place, seemingly without partners. Explosions of laughter burst out as the alcohol took hold. Men and women sometimes paired up and disappeared. I estimate that at least half of the household found themselves teeming with energy those first months and inclined to spend it.

Because of the aims set before us, Bennett made one rule: the exclusion of drugs. I never saw this rule broken that year. There was, however, plenty of drinking, except during periods when we collectively observed periods of abstinence.

As most of the students were young and unattached, a fair number of liaisons formed as soon as people began to arrive. Sexual stimulation was abundant, and our coed living conditions maximized the opportunity, although privacy could be a problem. Generally, all this was discreetly conducted, but certainly prevalent.

The influx of pubcrawlers from the school became somewhat of a problem for Sherborne villagers, who were unfairly outnumbered. After a few evenings of social intermixing with the Sherborne House residents, the villagers sequestered themselves around two or three tables at one side of the clubroom. Our buoyant chatter allowed few openings for shared experience. When the second course came the following year, Bennett instructed Mick Sutton to set up a bar in the main library and tend it for an hour each evening whereby the household could drink and socialize in the open. This effectively returned the public house of Sherborne village to its rightful clientele while providing the means for containing our collective behavior and energies within the house itself.

As the year drew on, the number and attendance of the after-hours gatherings diminished. We began to acquire the taste for conserving our states. Something was meant to build up between us as a group and inside each of us individually, and it was not long before we saw this happening. Also, we had very little free time throughout the long day, and the body wanted to sleep. But for the first months, the novelty of our life together, the sexual attraction, and the surplus energy that our daily regimen produced made after-hours carousing and late night conversations in private rooms, over beer and sherry, a regular event. Although a number of us had but a few hours sleep, just before dawn virtually everyone was seated again in the ballroom, waiting for Bennett to appear and lead us through the next morning exercise.

CHAPTER ~ SEVEN

THE FIRE WAS going when we entered the ballroom each morning. Manfred's unmoving shape greeted the earliest arrivers from its post. Bolt upright, barrel-chested, he sat cross-legged with palms on knees, before the chamfered corner of an alcove, like a bronze Lohan. Fresh from our cold water ablutions, we entered one by one, found a cushion and silently took the same position. There were few chairs in the house; we were accustomed to sit on the floor during all of our other meetings as well, but rather more lax. Manfred, however, would not slacken his body for an instant. He spoke his excellent, German flavored English without gestures or mannerisms, with hardly a blink. The effect was disconcerting for someone like me, who was given to fidgeting while speaking. Manfred seemed to be the very embodiment of self-containment by comparison.

When the dervish, Hasan Sushud, came for his visit, he noticed Manfred seated among us and turned to Bennett to ask, "Why is that fellow sitting like a Yogi?"

Bennett waited for Manfred to speak for himself. I no longer remember the soft-spoken, probing exchange, except that Manfred did not bat an eye throughout, nor slacken his posture.

Hasan ended by telling Manfred that he needed to become "lighter" inside, as I remember. That would be his work. Even unwavering self-discipline needs balancing. Everyone needed to find their own work. My own work had to do as well with self-containment: I had too little of it.

SITTING STILL is a tough assignment. Morning exercise required one to sit as straight as possible, first of all in order to remain awake. But a cross-legged position was impossible for me to maintain. The leg underneath invariably went to sleep, and I would have to recross or straighten it until circulation reasserted itself.

Bennett, on his cushion, set his watch on the floor. Not once did he adjust his legs, for the entire hour. I thought this was extraordinary for a seventy-three-year-old body. The elders of our household used chairs, which Manfred set out for them, to sit "Egyptian style."

Fresh from our cold water ablutions, we entered silently in stocking feet, found a cushion and a place to sit. The women sat on one side of the long ballroom, two or three rows deep. Facing opposite was the same arrangement of men.

The long room was ringed in black statuary.

Morning exercise was a sort of calisthenics, done inwardly. The first distinction between these exercise and other forms of meditation is that they are practiced with eyes open. The elements of these exercises, theoretically, could be practiced anywhere.

I felt like I had entered kindergarten, to rediscover a world closer than my own flesh. Words like "sensing" and "feeling" were used, for the first time in memory with an idea behind them to give them meaning. By sensation, Bennett implied an actual substance, having physical-like properties such as viscosity, portability, and so on. He gave us a couple of hints for what to look for, and we began seeking it in the body's extremities where it is more readily detectable.

He directed us to put our attention into the right hand. "Put" is an accurate way of expressing it: we easily make the mistake of "thinking" our attention, that is, forming a mental image of the object instead of directing our attention upon it. It's like picking up an object, transporting and depositing it in another location. I knew I was there when sensation made its own response.

Bennett took us through a number of experiments with this newly objectified aspect of ourselves. I confirmed that it was mobile, stretchable, having its own, slow pace that could not be hurried. I experimented with drawing sensation up my arm, filling it like a vessel. This mobility allowed other experiments to be made. Having filled my arm with sensation, I lifted it slowly off my knee, held it out, bent it at the elbow, rotated the forearm upward and pointed straight-armed to the ceiling. I slowly brought my hand back to my knee. Then Bennett had us repeat the gestures, with "sensation arm" only. It was a strange dual physicality: to experience the ghost of my own arm detaching itself and shoving off into the stream to perform on its own.

After a few weeks I was aware of the sensation of my body growing. The circuit in my body was at first discontinuous, with pockets of sensation adjacent to null regions. We worked at different exercises for arousing and strengthening sensation, with the aim of forming, as it were, a body within a body. Every two weeks Bennett changed the exercise but all of them relied on sensation to one degree or another. He called these first exercises, "soil preparation."

I discovered sensation to be a direct means of perceiving how one's body is related to its surroundings. As winter came on and ice formed on the walks, Anna Durco suggested to us that we evoke sensation in our feet for walking over the hazardous surfaces. When I tried this, my body seemed to be acutely connected to the conditions underfoot. I pictured my sensation body lifting off the ice, conferring a peculiar upward pull to my physical weight, somehow more transparent to gravity. This strange, yet convincing, impression was typical of the quasi-material world of sensation. It was at this level, Bennett claimed, that we find an interface between the world of bodies and the world of spirits.

Feeling was not nearly so easy to objectify as sensation. For one, feelings reverberate within the brain, filling it with pleasant images or angry thoughts wanting to be spoken. Feelings like fear, irritation, or embarrassment register in the face. Fourth Way psychology sides with popular wisdom, that feelings originate in the solar plexus. I looked for some evidence of this when I felt my emotions aroused. Sometimes my heart literally jumps in my breast, sometimes I ache, but just as often the physiological reaction could lodge elsewhere in my body. I was struck by how little I knew of my own psychophysiology.

Bennett said that the center of our emotions can hardly be called a center at all. In fact, part of our internal disharmony is due to the decentralized structure of our so-called "feeling apparatus," dispersed as it is throughout the trunk of the body: the ganglionic array. Nevertheless, it is a specialized and finely tuned organ of perception, whose operations are mercurial, especially when compared to the thinking function. I could not distinguish a feeling from my own reaction to it; with the feeling center, one thing followed the other, as if cut from the same cloth.

Morning exercise very soon called upon the feeling center's participation. We directed attention into the solar plexus to awaken a feeling of "inner emptiness"—something akin to remorse which, Bennett suggested, comes by contemplating lost opportunity, the squandering of the time allotted to us. This might be perceived as a kind of ache, or a void in our chest which wants to be filled. Whatever it was that we would come to by this effort, we were to keep part of our attention on it and an equal part of it on our sensation body.

These "morning exercises" treated thoughts, feelings, and sensations as if they were transportable materials. The longing in our breast could be directed into a limb and allowed to blend with the sensation. The energy of the "head-brain" could be transported into the breast, and so on. The brain itself got a work-out: it had to hold the pattern of the exercise, divide and follow attention, make the steps of the exercise happen. It also had the additional burden of struggling with frequent drowsiness.

This head brain had its own muscles to be developed, and one of them was integral to other exercises. We began by projecting a thread of energy from our forehead and directing it at various targets. We projected mental images out, and drew others in, through this thread. It reminded me of the difference between imagining a subject and focusing on it to the exclusion of everything else.

Our education in this second sight began with a tiring "nine-point exercise," where the thread was fed out to the right foot. With the connection made and the thread pulled taut, the mind was to travel down the thread with the aim of residing there and experience "being a foot." Bennett patiently dwelled on these efforts for long minutes, then cued us to draw our foot up the thread into our head and hold it there for more long minutes.

This was about as entertaining as sit-ups. The flagging brain had to be revived by a breathing exercise before moving to the next point on the circuit around the body. It required an inordinate amount of struggle with sleepiness and produced no gratification whatsoever.

Bennett encouraged us to report our observations in performing the exercises. One student offered up this admission: "I think I am actually having success with it. But I must say, I really don't like having my foot inside my head." Bennett laughed in pure pleasure. "Yes, it is like that! It can be peculiar, this inner world ... where it is possible for us to feel curiosity in, say, our left foot." We laughed, knowing what was coming next.

After moving to the longer exercises of the coming months, I realized I could not have attempted them without this mental workout. This feeding out of a mental thread was put to various uses, for contacting anything from material objects to a projected mental image of reservoirs of grace or other higher influences. With this thread we swept the room, contacting everyone present, then directed our mental threads to a common vortex above us. Bennett's desire to establish a bond between us became plain as the sessions advanced. We closed an exercise with offering part of our work to our common presence.

To remind us of our purpose, we made three offerings while bowing from the waist. The first third of the results of our efforts was offered as food for our own being; the second, for all life; and the third, for "That which lies beyond All." Sometimes the third offering was stated as for "the Work."

THE EXERCISES soon began showing themselves as friendly forces. I have only to remember a single occurrence not two months from the start of the course:

An impromptu movements class with all ninety students drew to a close. Bennett signalled for us to sit and then explained how to do Number Thirty-Nine.

This movement differs from others in that most of it is internalized. Each round signals a move from sensing, to feeling, to thought. In the first gesture, palms were on knees; In the second and third gestures, one, then the other, palm is placed across the breast; in the fourth gesture the head bows. A pattern of three inner and four outer positions: twelve combinations.

The slow tempo made this simple division of attention hard to sustain. My mind wandered until a change of hands brought me back. By returning again and again to sensing my body, it became fully shaped, able to maintain itself even when my attention lapsed. My brain cleared of rambling thoughts and chatter. The seven long chords for each position were like eternity made present.

Like a light switching on in a dark room, a golden current of emotion streamed out of my chest and bathed every atom of me and around me. I felt existence itself! The next chord called hands back to knees. The gushing flood found its level and became a still pond, at the center of which was the undoubted presence of I Am!

THIS MOMENT THAT I have just described was like a coming out of a jail in which my mind and soul had been confined in separate cells. Out of the blue, here I was—wholly here! No inner exercise or special music could simulate such an experience. It was not that I had come to a "state" which could be subtracted from or added to. Rather, I had come to what I was: an ephemeral, localized monad of the living, conscious cosmos. Everything suddenly mattered. I felt privileged to be able to want to work.

That burst of affirmation lasted for about three weeks.

Most everyone had experiences of this kind, and more than once. Each would witness their own ineluctable decline back into the inertial sludge. Bennett endeavored to show us it was possible to put all experiential extremes to practical use, rather than merely enjoy to dissipation or suffer without understanding, and pointed to the fact that they each are one end of the same stick.

The rhythms of affirmation and denial informed the way the basic course was managed. Bennett partitioned the year into weekly phases, each devoted to a special subject of study. We had five days and nights to make something of these special assignments, called "themes", before they were abandoned. Regardless of one's degree of performance, the work would be approached fresh every Monday morning.

CHAPTER ~ EIGHT

WE DISTINGUISHED SENSATION from feeling, attention from thinking. There would be other shades to explore: intentionality, wholeness, other people, present moment, seeing versus noticing, self-will versus willfulness. No formal definitions were offered. We had, instead experiences bearing on the subject, which every Friday night we witnessed to Bennett.

Theme meetings were frequently an ordeal. Speaking up before everyone about our modest awakenings was a show-and-tell we would instinctively avoid. It turned out that we had little to hide, a fact as belittling to the ego as anything could be. What felt worse—I frequently felt it—was coming to the Friday night discussions with nothing to give. The crop-picker back from the field with an empty bag.

Bennett was extremely resourceful in finding nuggets in our meager contributions. In fact, any presentation made to sound interesting he slapped down instantly. Thanks to the general rule only to report actual observations, I gradually lost my concern over what others would see when I spoke. All the same, I trembled inside while waiting to signal Bennett that I wished to speak. What were these themes meant to produce?

"We have to set ourselves to add a dimension to our experience," he offered, "to become able to perceive the height and depth of experience, and not merely its successiveness or its spread around us. For this we have to accept and be convinced that there is depth, that there is more in simple things than meets the eye, or more than can be described in language."

The first theme he gave was easy to get into: Awareness of material (inanimate) objects. All week long I encountered man-made tools and utensils communicating their nature and purpose. I sensed qualities in materials by their feel, their sound underfoot, and so on. I felt like my own senses were being raised to another power; we all did, as our delightful first theme debriefing made clear. During this open meeting, Bennett made an observation I have not forgotten. Our coming into contact with the material world, he said, is for us an ascent to a higher world; not, as we usually think of it, a descent into a lower one.

Some themes could be extraordinarily enabling, like that of the fifth week, which required an effort I had believed was beyond me. He called it "separation from the polarity of like and dislike" and suggested we undertake for experimentation the following: when we find ourselves in a position of choosing between something we like and something we dislike, we choose the latter.

All week I had resources at my disposal for meeting annoyance with patience, adversity with tolerance, self-gratification with impartiality. This was obviously a temporary state of affairs, I told myself; it was far too easy. As suspected, my new powers fizzled at the midnight hour. The weekend came, with the opportunity to enjoy my customary indulgences, now restored to sovereignty just because the mechanism of the theme had been officially "closed" the night before! The theme was not only a foretaste of inner freedom, but hard evidence of a preference for pleasure. But there was an important difference: by breaking the pattern of always doing what I was inclined to do, I saw how insubstantial and imaginary most of my dislikes really were. When I chose to shoulder something, my opposition to it lost its grip and slipped away for a while.

A week's work on a theme did not guarantee revelations. More often I encountered my own psychological insecurities, my indolence, my essential immaturity. But theme meetings were not psychological counseling sessions, and Bennett cut short any attempt to make them so. His way of doing this was not gentle: quick to perceive what was coming, he stopped the student in mid-sentence with a blunt admonition and then picked someone else to speak. In fact, he could cut you off for no apparent reason and pick someone else out to speak.

About themes, I ran into a personal problem: I perceived that I was failing at working with themes. I was greatly confused between what I was in fact perceiving and my thoughts about what I was perceiving, how I was perceiving (was I doing it right?), and so on. I watched this grow into a larger dilemma than it should have been; it hindered effort and fed something morosely doubtful in me. Obviously this was not what theme study was about. I finally formulated the problem to Bennett in one of the meetings in this way:

"I have come to the conclusion that I don't really know what an observation is. I have gotten myself into a position where I don't even know if I could recognize one."

"Give me an example."

"When I remember the theme, I want something to happen. Then I think that desiring something to happen will just get in the way. Now I am no longer concentrating on the theme, but wondering if anything will come to me before the week is over. And then I start doubting my sincerity, seeing myself worrying that I will have nothing to say at the next theme meeting ..."

Bennett hesitated for a long moment, then settled back into his chair. "You think too much." I waited for him to say more. "This is not really thinking at all, of course; just brain activity. The next time you find yourself doing this, sense your hands."

Then he addressed everyone: "A theme is not some idea to merely think about. Working on any theme is to become attuned to the opportunities around us for the theme to manifest. The theme should be a way of life, for that week."

This advice did not make theme study any easier for me, but it made it possible. I also learned to better differentiate mental excretion from active thinking.

Certain moments in theme meetings are recalled in this book. Such moments lose most of their content in the transcription. Bennett validated or dismissed our contributions not so much according to their content but rather as to how we were while delivering them. To read or listen to a recorded theme meeting confuses the commentary with the action, lurching from the dire to the comic, always courting the element of surprise.

I remember Bennett telling a joke-parable about two dervishes, one fat and the other thin, who were cast ashore on a tiny island without food or drink. One survived the other. The punch line had a twist, but Bennett made use of a pronoun ambiguously, with the result that I was not sure which dervish was supposed to have been the survivor. I sensed from the room that others were also doubtful. I raised my hand and pressed the point: "Pardon my slowness, Mr.B., but … which one was it that survived?"

This released an explosion of laughter from Bennett as well as everyone else. Then he looked at me and asked, "Which one do you think?" I gave a flustered answer that in fact I expected was incorrect. "The fat one?" Bennett's beaming face transformed into cool displeasure. My self-satisfaction turned to humility without missing a beat. The unthinking response confirmed how my intention and my speech can be so unlinked. This habit of leaping forward with the wrong answer, it turns out, is one which I still need to watch with vigilance. That moment was when I first became aware of it.

THE MAJORITY OF THEMES were not introspective but looked outward. The theme of noticing, for instance, turned our egocentric orientation inside out: rather than perceive the world outside as an extension of myself, I felt what it is to be an extension of what exists around me. The difference between seeing and noticing an object or condition was contact. "We know we are in contact with something when we perceive its needs, its own claim to sustenance and care. We feel ourselves becoming second to that other."

All that week I looked around and saw many things which a modest effort would improve. The household seemed to attain a higher level of order everywhere I looked. More significantly, I felt the presence of all of us together as more than a gathering of people, but a conscious, complex organism for bringing intelligent management to the world. Quite naturally, the taste of stewardship brought us to wonder how so much social illness and famine in the midst of plenty would be mitigated by a shift in attitude!

The theme for the eighth week was food. We saw Bennett's opinion of our egoistic discriminations over what is and is not worthy of our consumption. "All food is good, if we eat it in the proper state. We should receive food like an honored guest, cognizant of all the work that has been done by Great Nature to bring it to us. We should be heaven for the food we eat, where it is transformed upward to a higher level of energy."

A breakfast cook described his wonder at seeing raw grain turn into porridge. This brought forth from Bennett a startling new perspective on the subject:

"It is very strange that we take so little notice of the fact that nature provides food which animals can readily eat, but that we alone find it necessary to take it a step further by bringing it into contact with fire. The wonder of this has disappeared through familiarity. All the anthropologists' explanations of how man came to use fire really disregard this mystery. Our precursors were capable of eating raw food in various ways, but as time passed, we learned to transform meat by direct contact with fire and later discovered bread baking, which is yet more wondrous. When we see the action of the yeast transforming the bread, we begin to understand why through the centuries bread has been given a special respect.

"How and why did all this enter our lives? Because the energies that man must produce are different from those required of other animals, and the action of the fire has to make its contribution. What you saw is a mystery. We need to be able to see the mystery in familiar things, such as this strange thing, that the preparation of food before eating is integral with human life, and that this preparation practically always involves bringing energy to bear. If we do not use fire, we cut and pound and stir, and this energy also transforms. When we (at Sherborne) began cooking for ourselves, our potatoes sometimes reached us half-cooked, and we recognized that by mashing the potatoes with a fork, we could put in more energy to make the transition between the raw and the cooked potato more complete."

As I said, we were discouraged from pursuing special diets for other than medical or religious reasons. Someone finally asked for his straightforward opinion of eating a balanced diet.

"There are physiological effects from an unbalanced diet. Moreover, every kind of food contains a certain psychological nourishment: rice eaters and bread eaters have recognizable differences, as do fish eaters and meat eaters.

"Many things about the effects of different food that were once known are now forgotten. There was a time when the infusion of the coffee bean was a ritual. Now we drink it constantly as a kind of stimulant, no longer mindful of its significance—that a particular alkaline in the coffee corresponds with our blood and is therefore able to pass a message and produce a particular state. There are even things we now use for the exact opposite of their original purpose. The real use of alcohol is to strengthen in people their own wish; now it is used to get rid of feelings of remorse, or to feel comfortable with oneself, or just to stimulate.

"The evolutionary process that has taken two or three thousand million years to establish itself on the earth's surface reaches us all the time through food. By far the greatest part of the transformational activity on the earth is made by vegetable and invertebrate life. Everything that all higher forms of life feed upon is first prepared in the vegetable world. And we who subsist in the midst of all this, do we suppose it all stops with us?

"It cannot be so: the transformational exchange must pass through us and serve for higher purposes. The great difference between us and all other forms of life on Earth is our possibility of doing this consciously. This is what it means to be human. To eat without being aware of the significance of food is subhuman, the way animals eat."

Bennett closed with one of his rare injunctions: "You should always try to remember the significance of food: by remembering this you will look at things in the right way and come towards an understanding—a painful understanding—of love. Just stop a minute and consider how many things in the world would change if the responsibility involved in taking life were actually understood, and how a different value system would emerge for the whole of humanity. We cannot evade this responsibility by quibbling, 'I won't eat vertebrates but I will eat vegetables.' Whatever we eat, we are taking life, and we have the responsibility for converting that life into conscious energy."★ Although the theme fostered a different attitude in me towards eating, losing myself in its pleasure was always a temptation. Our communal eating first served as a reminding factor; but as the ritual became familiar, its effect wore thinner. There was, however, a grace we sometimes said over meals which always reminds me of food as sacrament:

All Life is One, and everything that lives is holy.
Plants, animals, and men, all must eat to live and nourish one another.
We bless the lives which have died to give us our food.
Let us eat consciously,
Resolving by our work to pay the debt of our existence.

Thanksgiving, Bennett warned, will work for two or three weeks or even months, but eventually becomes a routine; people's minds will be occupied with something quite irrelevant. External reminders act only on a very superficial part of us. The force to go against the stream must eventually come from ourselves.

I BEGAN THIS chapter by claiming Sherborne to be a place where words lost ambiguity. But certain objects of our concern were inherently paradoxical. No one can define what having one's own "I" means. The feeling of "I" in my breast seemed to draw toward what lay beyond itself—rather like a cloud appearing, then evaporating. There was this impulse to be re-absorbed into the source of everything, coexisting with the urge to consolidate what there is of me. Selfhood is very important; it is the place where we live.

A student of Bennett's from Coombe Springs days, John Wilkinson, told a small gathering of us that the prospect of gaining one's own "I" was really just a hook which Gurdjieff tossed out to get people's interest. "There is no such thing as a permanent 'I.' But to know this does not mean you have understood anything. See how it is here in the school: Dick Holland proves in his psychology

★ Bennett's comments on food were recorded and later published in: *The Sherborne Theme Talks* , vol. 4 (1977: Coombe Springs Press). These books are long out-of-print.

class that man has no 'I', nor will, whatsoever. Then you meet with JGB, who says that man can do and can experience his own 'I.' You are left to work this out for yourself. Absolutely no one can do it for you."

The domain of the work is described as paradoxical by nature: where many things are true as well as their opposite. Bennett coined a few memorable examples, like this favorite of mine: Sometimes the impossible becomes possible by increasing the difficulties.

clockwise from top left: Elizabeth Bennett; Bhante: The Venerable Vira Dharmawara, in Asoka Vihara, India, 1971. (Photo: Sally Massa) ; Virgil Walker, student; Gerald Wilde, artist in residence.

clockwise from top left: "Mr. B"; JG Bennett observing movements classes in the Great Hall (Photos: Diane Cilento).

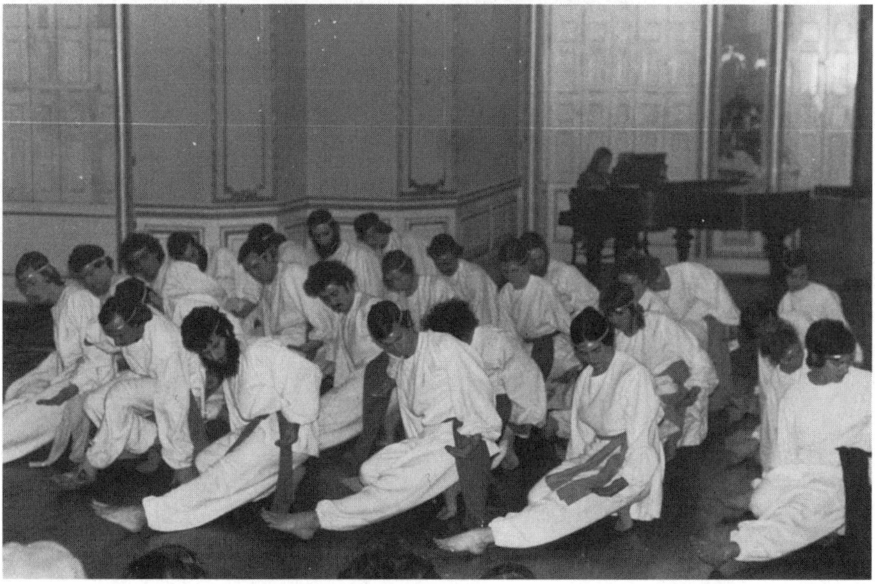

Sherborne House Movements Performance. *top:* "a class waiting to begin." *bottom:* performing "The March Forward," Number 5 of the "obligatory" series of movements.

A Sherborne House Movements Performance of "Camel Dervish Prayer."

clockwise from top right: Sally Massa; Lynn O'Brien; Moshe Siev; Eric Davis, at the controls; Trilby Noon; Mick Sutton.

Rick Margolin reading the prayers for Passover. To his left: Michael Jasnow, Moshe Siev

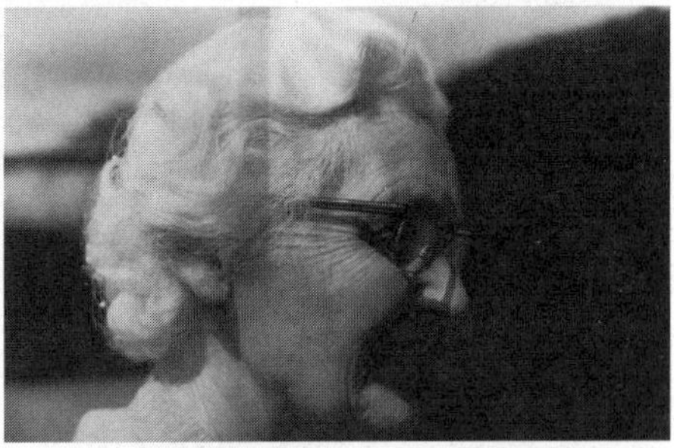

clockwise from top right: Sharon Walker; Lili Helstinius, senior member of the Bennett circle, was "great aunt" and friend to many Sherborne students; Charlotte Janis and Bruce Epstein; Richard Duffell, the eldest of those who came; Tim St. Claire Ford; Jane Cole with son Jason.

clockwise from top left: Miss Olga de Nottbeck, senior member of the Bennett circle, tended the enneagram rose garden through five courses; the rose garden in 1975, (postcard); Students skinning turf for the enneagram rose garden. (photo: courtesy of Allen Roth)

clockwise from top: Dining room, with Dutton family portraits keeping watch. Meals were dumbwaitered to the servery beyond; Gerald Wilde, bohemian character and world famous contemporary artist, in his studio at Sherborne House talking with a close friend visiting from Rumania. (photo: Gerald Green); Gerald Green (left), Sherborne Village Building Inspector, meets George Cornelius, one of Bennett's senior circle, at the front of Sherborne House, 1970. The two were to become close friends.

clockwise from top left: Mr. and Mrs. Bennett along stone ornament (gift of Idries Shah,) the day before his death. (photo: Avis Rappaport-Licht); Mick and Laurence Sutton in 1979, (photo: courtesy of Laurence Sutton); Anthony Blake, dressed for Morris Dancing at one of the Sherborne fetes. (photo: courtesy of Allen Roth)

CHAPTER ~ NINE

MR. HOLLAND TAUGHT Fourth Way psychology, with detours into his historical interests. This courtly gentleman was near Bennett's age, with a voice unsteadied by a past illness. He appeared each morning in necktie and vest, silver hair straight over his scalp, bearing an easel, large diagrams and tables done in fine calligraphy.

Holland was very approachable. We both found common enthusiasms, for mathematical curiosities and fine draftsmanship. He showed me his drawing desk and pens. He loaned me an interesting textbook he used to teach math in public school, showing structural correspondences between the piano keyboard, the genealogy of bees, and the equiangular form of the nautilus. He was a scholarly man, devoted to Bennett, and made use of Bennett's book, *A Spiritual Psychology* for his discussions on St. Augustine.

Holland was soft-spoken but relentless on a few points, especially the centerpiece of Fourth Way psychology—we cannot do; we have no will; everything merely happens to us. This is a rather grim point of departure for a spiritual teaching.

By contrast, Bennett was the optimist. Man's true destiny is to participate in the domain of realization.

One of us confronted the issue head on. "Dick," he interrupted, "when I finish speaking, I will stand up." After a short pause, he stood up. "Can you say that I did not just now do anything?"

Mr. Holland looked at him for some time and then asked, "On what scale would you place this act of will of yours?"

BENNETT INTRODUCED DOING as the theme for the seventh week. He defined doing as acting from one's own initiative and gave us a task which required just that. Once every hour we were to "collect ourselves" and to keep a faithful record of our success throughout the week. In a day or two, I found myself remembering to check the hour just before it was about to strike! After this high point passed, it then became increasingly harder to sustain. At the end of the week, we reported our experiences and observations, during which Bennett concluded:

"We can do, but we must first satisfy three requirements: that our intention is presented in a clear mental form; that by working on ourselves we are producing the required energy; and that we have a real wish to do it."

He had indicated a turn in the road ahead, then left the subject for a fortnight, until he introduced a theme called "irrevocable decision." For this theme, he made it clear, there can be no failure. Then he proceeded to lead us through the steps—seven in all—of the "decision exercise." It was an integral part of everything which would follow for the rest of the year.

All of our morning exercises finished with a space of time for taking the decision. Making the commitment to myself, as it turned out, was the opposite of assertiveness; it was purely receptive. I asked from a still, patient, prepared state, if this decision had been "given to me" and waited for an answer. "If the answer is no," Bennett said, "you must accept it and try again tomorrow."

First experiments were to be simple and unambiguous: shining one's shoes, folding laundry, writing a letter, and the like. The task itself was the easy part. The hardest came at the end. By this stage of the course, the long days left our bodies weary and eager for sleep. It was at the last moment before going to bed, that the last two of the seven steps finally came.

The first of these, the retrospect, consisted of comparing the image and the performance. There would be a consequence, had this mental comparison not accorded with the decision in all essentials, in the form of a day-long fast, holding my arms out sideways for several minutes, a cold bath, or any harmless thing which reminded my body that it would be the one to pay. Holding one's arms out sideways for eight or ten minutes quickly recruited my body into service.

The retrospect was followed by choosing tomorrow's decision. The process began by noticing conditions around me that needed tending, or improvement, or beautification. Is this action appropriate? Is it feasible?

Only after that was settled, could we go to sleep. There was always the temptation to rush through this last part. But it was the last conscious act of the day, and so became its emblem and seal. It was difficult not to want to make a respectable effort of it.

BENNETT ASKED US to identify a personal mannerism or habit which served no essential purpose—habitual gestures while speaking, for instance—and convert the force of this habit into a reminding factor for doing it in some other way, or putting another action in its place. Decisions were not formulated as "Thou shall not," but as "It shall be done this way, rather than that."

I began to see the possibility of harnessing the opposing forces within me for a purpose. Many of us showed signs of champing at the bit. This person wanted to quit smoking, that one to lose weight. We wanted to test it out on the big things. Bennett said that what he hoped for us was only in its germination.

The tobacco users among us soon got their wish to work with the habit. Bennett gathered the smokers into a special group. He reminded us that our first struggles would produce a negative substance, which can, however, be neutralized by a certain kind of breathing.

This chemistry proved effective. When we met again with Bennett, he encouraged us to begin eliminating any compensatory indulgences we naturally acquired from this struggle. Biscuit and candy sales at the Sherborne Village store had skyrocketed.

"Those of you who have habits like smoking," Bennett said, "or indulging in sweets, alcohol, and the like, have a particular advantage at this stage of your work. This way of transformation requires a certain amount of struggle, not for its own sake, but for setting up an action under which things begin to change. To have some easily perceived weakness in oneself is like having a foothold from which we can raise ourselves. Many of you have no such obvious habits or indulgences and must, therefore, search further in yourselves for patterns of behavior to serve as your denying force."

The decision exercise could be interpreted as behavior modification. It was, by my experience, a pathway into a clear area where conscience can be petitioned. This was the best expression of the aim of the course, as Bennett said on opening day.

I had been putting off answering a letter from a friend who was curious to know what we were doing. I contemplated a bubbly sketch of Sherborne's supercharged pace. But then I saw how ordinary it all would sound. The description of a day in the life? We practice a moving yoga; we meditate; we fast and observe silent days; we suck cold water up our noses ... "And?" I heard my correspondent asking. Her letter lay there on my writing table for weeks.

When I finally made it a decision to answer it, the day was one of liberation. Sitting down to write the letter that evening was like stepping into a niche carved in time; like a coat held out for me.

We experimented with our ways of relating to other people. The dynamics of the school changed considerably. We involved one another in private, pre-planned interactions. "No one," Bennett cautioned, "must bear the smallest price for your decision. It should be a secret; but, if you suspect you are playing a part in someone's effort, for our purposes you should cooperate with them. You must be clever about this. You must allow for people's unpredictability when you plan your decision, and be clear that your own part can be carried out." This amounted to a performance, prepared beforehand and carried out as a decision.

Initial experiments were innocuous. People came up from behind and started unlikely conversations. I practiced keeping a straight face when someone's sociability was particularly transparent. Some of my prepared intercourses were also detected. Renato simply laughed when I caught him at the bulletin board. He recovered his composure and played along with my listless performance. I had not prepared for this well, I realized. I had dispensed with the decision as if it were one more item on my to-do list. I felt like I had forced him into my pantomime of a wind-up dummy pretending to be alive.

From such slipshod efforts, I realized that decision must be taken very seriously. I was reminding myself daily that we had but a few months left to us for working under these specially arranged conditions. It would be much harder afterwards.

WORK IN VISUALIZING tasks recruited the entire household to execute them, like preparing a weeded acre for planting and irrigation. We projected ourselves into the details, the stages of the transformation of the field, and into the significance of it. Bennett was keen on these experiments. He sometimes ventured to us that a special presence entered these special activities. Sometimes I felt nothing of the sort. But I also remember moments that stand outside the flow of time, having a unifying silence which hovered everywhere as if, as Sufis put it, "an angel had flown through the room."

Bennett spoke of the presence of Work, a blessed substance which certain kinds of conscious efforts attract. This overarching presence gave J.G. Bennett's school the feeling of a religious community.

Sally asked Bennett one day to teach her how to pray. Her family had not been religious, but reactionary in fact; for the first time in her life she felt a serious need for prayer. Bennett's reply was revealing: he told her that the decision exercise is prayer.

I had not described the making of decisions to my friend back home. I did not know then what this practice over time would eventually reveal: that we were learning how to pray. And in learning to pray, we were learning how to do. To speak openly and intelligibly at the time about what I was doing was pretentious. In the quarter century since, I have hardly found a context in which this side of our work at Sherborne could be mentioned. But of all the variety of experience afforded there, including the daily round of psychological and intellectual stimulation, nothing so characterized the life at Sherborne as this alighting of the sacred upon a simple act.

CHAPTER ~ TEN

INSTRUCTIONS TO COOPERATE with each other's efforts brought the household closer together. With the student body being shuffled and reshuffled, we felt more like an extended family. Families experience conflict, of course, and people push each other's buttons, violate egos that suddenly shrink, or rant in defiance. In short, the mesoteric stage of the course largely consisted of dealing with our own baggage.

"Why are you smiling like that?" Bennett asked Blaire one day. Blaire wore a pleasant, perpetual smile. He and Vakil were members of the Beshara group, a Sufi community which had established itself on a farm a few miles away at about the same time Elizabeth Bennett made an offer on Sherborne House.

Blaire was speechless. "I get tired of seeing you with that same smile," Bennett said coldly. "Do you imply that your inner state corresponds to this smile? Not even the most enlightened of men live in any such perpetual state." He may as well have told Blaire to wipe it off his face.

Bennett would confront anyone without warning, but never provoked a scene for affect. Being an upper-class Oxonian, histrionics were out of his range. He recognized that in many cases his own practiced formality would limit his program for all-round human study. People at certain times can benefit from getting their faces stretched.

To this end he persuaded a work group leader, John Allen, to bring his theater troupe, the Theater of All Possibilities, to Sherborne in the spring to shake us up, unmask our negativity, and act with it in a variety of creative situations. Allen's technique turned out to be helpful for some and revolting to others. Elizabeth Bennett distanced herself from the proceedings entirely.

But theater technique was no match for Bennett's withering bluntness. Such is demonstrated in the following journal entry of Lynn O'Brien:

> Sunday, February 27
>
> Much has happened but my memory is weak. It is as if I can remember nothing.
>
> We (P Group) had a second meeting with JGB during this week. He was not being easy with people. Roger made some question about not wishing to be crystallized as he was. JGB told him he was one of

the people here who he cannot reach, that Roger makes all the right efforts externally but will not do the one thing that will allow him to receive help.

Then I said that I still had come to nothing with the movements, that I was still copying and unable to work from myself, that I found my movements jerky and angular ... he interrupted me and spoke almost cruelly that I hadn't the slightest idea of what work was, I am full of self-love and this shows in the movements, it is an irritation to watch me, I am jerky and aggressive, I shouldn't be in this group, B didn't know why Anna insisted that I be put in the P group. He said "self-love," what seemed like many times. The reaction inside myself was one of revolt. I wanted to go away where these things about myself weren't true. He also said that he wondered if I'd ever be able to care about anyone other than myself. I don't recall anything much of the rest of the meeting. His tone was different with everyone that he spoke. He seemed harshest with me, perhaps equally harsh with Roger.

LYNN'S JOURNAL ENTRY continues on to the following Friday evening, after her initial confrontation with Mr. Bennett set things cooking all week:

Theme meeting on 25 Feb.: B allowed us our observations and did not comment on them individually as he says he won't do but usually does anyway. There were observations along the order of how true it is that we are mechanical. After about thirty minutes of this, I raised my hand to speak knowing that if I did not say what I had to say, it would eat at me for a long time. B had his eyes lowered but I saw that his eyes moved and he saw me. He turned his head almost directly around and called on Joe ... and after a silence I raised my hand again. He looked at me and I began to speak. I said that (in previous meetings) I found myself almost having something to say but before it could formulate itself into words, I had this sudden physical sensation of withdrawal and shutting myself in all over my body. Then my mind began with all sorts of excuses and reasons about not having anything to say. Then I saw what had happened and I began to see how this is what always happens. I come to a point when something is about to touch me, I withdraw ... I could see this recurring pattern in my life—how I wouldn't let my parents touch me, how in school I'd never ask questions or ask for help. ... And this immediate physical response to such situations surprises me, it is very animal-like.

When I was saying all this my voice was tight and I had to use force with myself to keep from crying. My eyes moved all around rarely looking at Bennett but when I did I could see that he was concentrating on me. When it was over he looked down and asked, "Does this picture

> that Lynn has painted of herself correspond to the picture you have of her?" and he looked around. I saw several heads nod and a few yea's and maybe two no's, one from George Cornelius. I did not catch what JGB next said, I did see that he shook his head. (Another student told her later that) B had said he did not think that was the way it was in a manner indicating that my observation may be valid but my conclusions are twisted. Moshe also told me that the ruthlessness with which I had said that I hadn't allowed my father to touch me shocked him. The whole tone with which I spoke seemed very cold. To me however, it was forced out with my emotions and it was all I could do to keep from crying, but I did feel detached from what I was saying as if it were about someone else. …
>
> On getting up this morning, Hermine told me that I had cried in my sleep and said, "Please don't," over and over. Laurie said that whenever she made a rustling I would whimper.

I WAS PRESENT at the two meetings she describes, but I remember Bennett's exchange with Roger somewhat differently. I may be mixing two memories together, but the incident was nevertheless instructive.

Roger expressed to Bennett that he was not sure how he should approach him—as an authority, a spiritual guide, leader of a movement, or what? Roger himself was an agile learner, physically and mentally, and was naturally motivated. He knew all the theory, he excelled in Movements during his time with the Gurdjieff Foundation, before coming to Sherborne. He made knowing and appropriate observations, posed relevant questions, put honest energy into every activity.

Bennett was cold in his reply. "You say all the right things, but it is all empty. You don't know how to relate to me because you don't need anything from me. The truth is, I can't help you." There was no caveat to this summation. He left Roger twisting in the wind.

However, I was of the opinion that Roger had orchestrated this confrontation. He was cutting ties. He had worked with the Gurdjieff Foundation and became disillusioned with the timid sheepishness of its membership, as he more or less expressed it to me. He came to Sherborne because Bennett might be different, an independent black sheep, who himself had struggled with the trappings of teacher-disciple relationships and was now opening his accumulated experience to all comers. Roger's radar was up when he arrived, sensitized to people's predilection for deferring to authority figures.

But Roger's skepticism was not especially out of place here. We all joked irreverently about "the great white elephant, JGB." One student dubbed Sherborne "the Bennetron," and that caught on for a while. I remember a group of wags, myself included, taking tea in the library and speculating on the equity realized by all the improvements we as tuition-paying students made to the place.

We marveled and winked at the cleverness of Bennett's eleventh-hour grab for a golden parachute.

Older hands had their stories as well. Mary Cornelius, one of the wartime residents of Coombe Springs, shared her recollection of Bennett in the businessman's role, cautioning me with sly amusement that certain people who had entered into partnerships with him found themselves holding the short end. "These leader-types may not necessarily look out for your interests at every turn," she smiled sweetly.

We absorbed the dirty linen and gossip, what there was of it, without shock. Everyone and everything became an open book, especially Bennett, who stood equidistant with us all. An entrepreneurial instinct attracted many of the males, a characteristic of Gurdjieff we found endearing. Most of us were still faced with making a material existence. I theorized that many of the single women were not oblivious to the demographics: if one is inclined to find a life-mate, why not look among those who want to "earn their living with their left foot?" They were attractive first, of course, because they were women, and because they were not silly. They were people willing to contemplate such a question as—How am I to face my own death if I can't even face a cold bath?

My own journal left a dismaying record of one-sided remorse and gnashing of teeth. At least there is truth in it, but it reads like a listless prison diary, whereas the days and nights at Sherborne were articulate and alive. Nevertheless, I read:

> April 21. Today I told Sally her constant criticism was destroying my self-image. She said my self-image was just the opposite: high, vainglorious; and the reason I was suffering was because all evidence, and not just her observations, was proving there was nothing inside of me to feel glorious about. This deflated me, because I agreed with it.
>
> I am having a hard time with craving stimulants and all my worldly pleasures. No desire to work, at anything; just give it all up, for a while. Yet, I never consider walking out of this! How does the state begin to lift? I expect and even look forward to returning to my old habits when I leave. No hope to free myself from the pull of the world. The philosophy is beginning to alienate me—sometimes angers me. Such skepticism is not producing anything, because it doesn't come from a wish for truth, but from hurt feelings, self pity, and disgust with having to go against my desires and hungers, and so on. This skepticism comes as a defense against anything that places demands on me.

What emerged from my journal was a bundle of unremitting negativity. The writer or witness is rather immature, obsessed with an inability to be a joyful person without medicating himself. What emerged from Lynn's journal was the self-image of a repressed youth, whose suspicion of other people was the baggage which came from her perception of being a worthless person. Neither of us, or anyone else at Sherborne, were disproportionately handicapped, of course. Fault lines began to show in everyone's composure, except those who by nature kept a studied countenance. The collective stress of our cloistered life came out in our jokes, our sudden run-ins with people, our sex life or lack thereof.

I continued to stew inside for weeks on end, until February when out of nowhere came a complete separation from my suffering selves:

> Reported to B in theme this morning, that I am suffering uselessly, because this kind of suffering does not increase my wish. My wish has left me. This negativity that I carry around with me probably results from not having wish, but it will not produce wish.
>
> B said this is a good place for me to be: if I had wish I would not be in the advantageous position of seeing my utter helplessness. He says it is possible from this point to make a step forward.

CHAPTER ~ ELEVEN

I HEARD IT SAID of the First Obligatory* that everything one could learn from movements could be had by executing this one precisely.

Beyond a handful of such lore, nothing was formally said about individual movements. Verbal instruction was brief and concrete, with no discussion of meaning or content. Each movement was a sort of dance, or ritual, said to be a little book to be read through the body. Each exercise brought a new set of challenges. More became revealed after coming to a stage where one's attention was no longer consumed by learning something unfamiliar.

We practiced the movements piecemeal, breaking off in the middle to take up something new. By returning to them for some time each day, we accumulated a repertoire of a dozen or more before Christmas arrived.

People who look smart and "together" were stripped of their composure right off. My self-regard became the first casualty of the engagement, and I soon learned it was best left at the door, like an orphan.

Anna Durco presented to us the ten arm positions of First Obligatory, following the next day with the same number of head and leg positions. Each sequence was relatively easy to execute separately. The difficulty was compounded by trying to put two of the series together. Attempting to combine the three was like hitting a brick wall, with my disembodied arms and legs flailing about like a harrow. My head flopped about its axis like a rag doll. Within seconds the effort short-circuited—my body would not respond. I was reduced to something less than zero.

My helplessness caused resentment. I was humiliated. I got angry. I got relaxed and got back into it again. "When you freeze up," Anna called out, "begin again as soon as possible." Emotional turbulence was there to be experienced: it belonged, but let nothing interfere with renewing the attempt. She was extremely business-like.

Nearly everyone managed to pull together the outward form of First Obligatory over the next few days or weeks. We were told, and it was true, that only by each of us practicing alone, could a group hope to bring one of the movements together. Anna seldom allowed us to continue for long at any exercise, even if we were showing signs of a breakthrough, but more often left

*The first movement in a series of six "obligatory" movements that prepared the student for other more advanced movements.

it for another new thing to practice.

I experienced flights of exhilaration after getting hold of a difficult pattern; and coherent messages passed between brain, body, and feelings, as when the bicycle I was learning to ride suddenly was upright and moving under my own propulsion; or gradually, by long practice, as in playing an instrument where one's fingers are hitting all the right keys. It was the taste of freedom, of being released from jail. At which time my eyes might lock onto the hips of my neighbor, the brunette. Sexual energy could be rampant in a movements class. The vigorous dervish dances set the room tingling with energy that could turn erotic with a little coaxing.

One movement called for the head to turn from right to left, left to right, while turning in place. The effect was strangely comical, looking alternately into each of my flanking partners' faces.

The effect of facing one another was raised to a level of poignancy in Number Twenty-One, or Remorse of Conscience. Each row began the continuous, flowing arm movement at a different point—straight to the front, then up, then out to each side, while bending at the waist from side to side and rotating to the four directions. While my arms were spread as if to receive, the person facing me extended theirs as if to pass an invisible current through me. The arms grew hot, like iron jabbed into a bed of coals, but the somber sweetness of the music made the pain almost cathartic. Each pose was a reception, a sampling, a letting go; an exchange of states among a carousel of rotating planets.

WHAT WE LEARNED of the origins of the movements was mainly hearsay. Movements were pieces of theater, which I first discovered when sitting out to watch others perform. Their far-flung themes showed the breadth of Gurdjieff's knowledge of old traditions and rites. When the range of these exercises is sufficiently understood through practice, movements prove to be a supremely demonstrable and practical psychological training program.

Among the bits of information circulated at Sherborne was a claim that there exist some three to four hundred fully choreographed movements from Gurdjieff. Ten months of daily practice allowed us to work at about fifty of them, together with quite a few nameless routines and exercises into which we were briefly plunged, never to return to them again.

There seems to be no available record of actual prototypes, or ethnological evidence of their previous existence. They arrived tailored to a classroom or studio situation with participants usually facing front in files and rows. Unlike the performing arts, only the dance itself and nothing of the performer's identity is interpreted or projected. Doubtless Gurdjieff had become very knowledgeable in the training of novices for temple rituals and native classical dance traditions. He had a flair for the stage and composed a ballet of movements which served to train students while presenting his Institute to the public. From this unpublished ballet, *The Struggle of the Magicians*, came one or two movements we ourselves would learn, namely: Number One, or Automaton, and Unfinished Obligatory.

Movements fall into groups or series', among them dervish and Tibetan dances, ritual dances, women's movements, obligatories—first and second series of six each, occupational movements (The Weaver and The Shoemaker are most charming movements for children), and the Series of Thirty-Nine. The last of this group of classic, fully choreographed movements was completed two weeks before Gurdjieff's death. There were to be forty in number, we heard.

Bennett himself told us he saw something resembling The Shahada, or Trembling Dervish, during his post-war years in Istanbul. The ceremony lasted all day and throughout the night with many of the dervishes continuing without a break. At the end of the ceremony, the Sheik called forward one of them to lie on the ground. A scimitar was placed on edge across the man's belly, upon which the Sheik balanced his full weight for several minutes without opening the flesh.

For this movement, men fanned out to claim an island of clear space for the sweeping arm positions and the tremulous chanting of "La illaha il' Allah." Arrayed in front, the women abandoned themselves to quaking improvisations.

A number of movements were ceremonial in character, often with separate parts to be taken by the women. For some reason the women's parts usually were far more difficult.

In Camel Dervish, we divided into a semicircle of men arrayed around a circle of women. The men's part was simple: one arm crossed the heart and then the other; we bowed from the waist, knelt and placed our foreheads on the floor; we rose, arms and eyes lifted to the ceiling.

Meanwhile, the women were executing a slow, fluid balancing act depicting a caravan of camels, desert ships, bells on wrists vibrating ceaselessly. Perched on one foot, their raised foot hovered, then pawed the earth on the downbeat. The foot lifted again, then dropped to receive the weight of the dancer, inching her way around the circle to the slow, potent music.

All the Tibetan movements had an unmistakable flavor: angular, ungainly body gestures that, with practice, revealed their alien beauty.

Canon of Seven was said to have come from the Essene Brotherhood. Others evoked Mithraic and Pythagorean imagery or Delphic expressions that audiences seemed to read instinctively. Some can only be described as prayers.

Gurdjieff set the composition of a movements group at six rows of six participants each, having in mind Chaldean arithmetic which acknowledges the aberrant behavior of number seven by taking six as its base. Canon of Seven therefore called for seven rows, to represent the seven-tone scale, do through si.

Movements sessions commenced on the first day of the course and continued ever afterward. I was astonished at the range and number of movements we could execute by summer of 1972, for they required an uncommon level of persistence which I would never have marshaled alone.

Eric Davis memorialized the dividing of the students according to their abilities. (Eric's group was the bottom rank.) Solemnly he declared, "P group will be performing Sharsi Varsi, Q group is doing Greek Letters, and R group will practice tying their shoe laces." It is the alien quality of some movements that highlight a central fact about biological existence: we are mobile units with movable appendages. Gurdjieff might have been indulging his impish sense of humor when composing movements like the Automaton, as if to exclaim, "Look here and see how we are: puppets on strings!"

Local visitors who chanced to pass by or walk in on these peculiar dance classes came away with impressions that left everything to their imaginations. One evening, Bennett attended a reception by local elders, clergy, and various county officials, resolved to have a look at Sherborne House's headmaster in person. Although this Bennett had noteworthy credentials, what were they to make of all the Yankee and London long-hairs (politics undeclared) comprising most of his student residents? What, for instance, was the purpose of the bizarre daily drill? Bennett accepted their invitation, shared cocktails and conversation, playing the headmaster, Army retired, with a respect for early morning constitutionals. He extended open invitations for them to observe the school activities first-hand or attend the open-house events held each Saturday. Leaving them reassured—there was no reason why they shouldn't be—he returned to Sherborne the same evening in time for theme meeting, where he related this to us. Relations between school and environs became steadily more open from then on. The local building official, Gerald Green, became a great admirer of Bennett and struck lasting friendships with many who came and went over the years of the Academy's existence. With reference to the public's perception of Sherborne, Bennett once said, "Sometimes a thing is disguised by appearing to be exactly what it is."

MOVEMENTS DO MORE than show our gears and cables. They also consist of rituals and dances and simple repetitive gestures which arouse many inner states, described approximately by words like devotion, offering, reception, supplication, submission, affirmation, forbearing, and so on. I recall Jacob Needleman's story, in *Lost Christianity,* of a wise Catholic priest who, when asked from where he thought the many spiritual psychologies and meditative practices might have come, replied that they were discovered by those who had observed their own states of being during prayer. Many of the movements are acts of prayer: wordless prayer, expressed through the physical body. The simple, archetypal gestures opened up feelings of reception and communion, so palpable that I could not but regard them as sacred. Cool water for the parched soul. I walked out of the movements hall many a time, feeling like I had just taken part in a timeless religious ceremony.

Bennett writes in *Gurdjieff, Making a New World,*⋆ that early dervish communities looked askance at the use of dance and music for inducing religious or mystical states. That was in the age when people identified themselves according to

⋆ Santa Fe: Bennett Books, 1992.

their faith. Everyone had prayers to say and rites to perform. There are vast populations who no longer do this. Gurdjieff's contribution was in bringing to the lapsed and moorless West a means for reopening people to the sacred in a direct way. He wanted people to appreciate and partake of their transcendental experience and understand their mechanicality, their states of relative and absolute sleep. Of all the variety of psychological and religious practices he found in his years of search, dancing became his chief specialty. His pupils found themselves recognizing states of being never experienced before, inner secrets hardwired in their neuroanatomy, experiences that passed through them from out of time and were gone, but never to be entirely forgotten.

Anyone who has worked with the movements (collectively referred to as Gurdjieff's "sacred dances") agrees that the less said about them the better. But the wall of silence surrounding the movements may run the danger of their being forgotten, which requires only one break in the line of transmission from teachers to students. You cannot have a school for movements* without people—eighteen or more, plus instructor and pianist. Without an influx of new people with a wish to work, this way of human development will be lost.

* Those readers interested in such a school should contact Bennett Books.

CHAPTER ~ TWELVE

ANNA DURCO WAS A contained mandarin presence who moved through our midst in unobtrusive silence. She observed with irony the peculiar brew of our community: the ingenuous familiarity of Americans testing the fastidious composure of the English. She was an American by birth herself, although one would not necessarily have guessed it. Her raven hair, gathered in a chignon, framed her face like smooth, folded wings. What little she telegraphed of her inner thoughts and feelings came through her eyes. She had distant eyes, dark red lips, high Mongol cheekbones. Always immaculately groomed yet comfortably dressed, she favored silk pantaloons, turtleneck, vest cut to the thigh, slender necklace.

Anna Durco, née D'urcova, was Slovakian and heard a number of languages spoken in her household. At the age of ten she chanced to meet Gurdjieff and conversed with him about his travels and his work in rich detail, in a patois of English, Russian, Romany, and assorted regionalisms which Anna was able to understand. She could have been an aristocrat by her comportment; half-gypsy or Magyar by her appearance. Her past was shrouded in mystery; she seldom spoke about herself or where she had been and learned. As the full-time teacher of movements, she was all business.

The warmth in her shined through when she saw a student hard in the struggle in one of her classes. Otherwise, she remained a cipher: aloof, never mixing, spending most of her free time in the privacy of her room. At meetings she sat somewhere on the periphery, in a cocoon of stillness. Somebody who had known her for years told me she had the skill for being invisible. This is true. I could never sense if and where she was in a large gathering: though a striking woman, my eyes would inexplicably pass her by unless I was looking for her intentionally.

No one, not Bennett himself, was exempted from her sudden, darting side-comments. Her unpredictable and oddly timed challenges pushed people's buttons. Someone sounded off in a meeting about this distraction: "She drives me up the wall," he admitted, "making it doubly difficult to concentrate." Bennett grinned, replying that he was all the more reassured of the wisdom in asking her to join him. She would, however, have a couple of famous confrontations with Bennett himself.

Women met with her in closed sessions, to practice "women's movements."

They put great demands upon the performers, in both the skill they exacted, and a corresponding inner detachment which, present or absent, determined the affect upon the audiences in our Saturday night demonstrations.

In these demonstrations I began to appreciate how it was for the Bennetts, Anna, and the other helpers, under the special conditions which we all had placed ourselves. A certain amount of role playing was fundamental to the assignments of students and instructors. In fact, role playing was officially part of the school curriculum. Learning to teach something we know to everyone else in the household was placed on all of us, which had to be organized by ourselves, absorbing every available work session for five weeks running.

Standing in squad formation before an assembly of strangers in our roomy white costumes girded in colored sashes, waiting eternally for the first chord of the next movement to strike, was the experience of bearing witness to the world at large, of a way of being which I resolve to work toward, of values I aspire to.

I liked Anna's ways, and the attitude she brought to the classes. It was said of her that as a performer of movements, she was perfection itself; but not once did she display her ability. She demonstrated positions and walked us through displacements, and as little of that as possible. I recall a moment when she brought her hands together above her head, fingertips touching. The movement was so fluid and the position so lapidary, it became engraved in my mind's eye. I knew then that she would have been an exquisite presence in a movements demonstration and regretted that I would not see it myself.

In the spring of that year, Bennett gave a public lecture in London. Those of us who signed on to attend and enjoy a day's outing before the evening lecture were shuttled in by a hired bus. After the lecture, Anna and I reboarded together, exchanging small talk while waiting for departure. She remarked that the lights inside the bus made it difficult to see out of the windows. I responded with one of those mindless, world-weary pronouncements people sometimes make when caught without anything to say: "Nothing going on out there worth seeing, anyway." "Oh, I see," she laughed and added dryly, "philosophy." Just the right pinch of irony to shrivel the ego. It was obvious that she had no compunction against an awkward rapport with someone confined next to her, even at the outset of a two-hour bus journey. On the other hand, she continued conversing with me as if the exchange had never happened.

In the last book Bennett published in his lifetime, *Gurdjieff: Making a New World,* Anna Durco is his most cited source for Gurdjieff's few, private disclosures about the movements and their origins. That book is full of interesting and obscure history about early dervish brotherhoods and lineages, but to my mind is highly speculative. Anna's written account of her meeting with Gurdjieff at the 1934 Chicago World Fair forms the basis for much of Bennett's conjecture:

" ... He told her his name and made her repeat it several times. He said that in the early spring many tribes of nomads and semi-nomads would pass through Kars not far from where he lived and some would camp near the Arpai Chai River. He said: 'I go see and find these people. I eat sometime and go together with the chavale (young boys). I go for many days from home. We sleep out under heavens. Three times almost caught for stealing, not valuable things, in bazaar. We ran-not catch. Such people *see,* can '*see.*' She recounts: 'He asked me if I knew what *drikérin mehétne* means. I knew the term from my father to mean foretelling the future and reading the past. He then told me that he ran off with a tribe of semi-nomadic Romanys who had come from the Carpathian Mountains and who were on the road to horse markets. He was eleven years old when he went with them. He added that although his father punished him severely, and although he loved his father, he could not help going because he learned many things from these people.'"*

BENNETT SPEAKS OF a school founded in twelfth century Turkestan by Ahmed Yesevi, who was trained as a Shaman alchemist but later became one of the eleven disciples and successors of Yusuf Hamadani—a Sufi "teacher of teachers" to whom several important dervish brotherhoods trace their origin. By Bennett's account, the Yesevis, more than any other Sufi community, developed music and rhythms that act directly upon the body and emotions. Sacred dances and music from pre-Islamic times were preserved by the Yesevis, and their psychological techniques, he thought, probably owe much to the Shamanist schools which flourished in the region. Even Yesevis of this century were regarded with suspicion by orthodox Sufi brotherhoods because of their close connections with Tibet and China. On the matter of Gurdjieff's connection with the Yesevis, Bennett's only citation is, again, Anna Durco:

"... When speaking of folk dances, he said that in Tashkent (which he pronounced Djashkent) there were special dances, but that further away there were very very special dances. Before one could see these one had to have a *palalikanina* which both in Sanskrit and Romany means 'a sponsor.' There they taught the Yesevi (pronounced by Gurdjieff Yiesef) dances and he had found a teacher who could teach by dancing what others taught by books. He said that only very very few people had the capacity to read the language of symbols. He then made a most significant statement—extraordinary for anyone, but strange indeed made to a child who fortunately remembered it word for word. 'In one place symbol, in another technique and in another dance.' ... (Yesevi) teach dancing same as put seed in the ground, but seed very hard, this green plant grow slow because need much time to grow, need very long time to give fruit, even much water will not help grow. Sometime this hard seed stay in ground for a long time—when begin to grow, change everything, all landscape can change. When symbol and technique grow together then give another plant, then grow quick and for other purpose. Special dance—sacred—very few can do. When symbol, technique, dance come in one place—then dance sacred for very special purpose."**

* J.G. Bennett. *Gurdjieff: Making a New World.* Santa Fe: Bennett Books, 1992, p. 16.
** ibid. pp. 79-80

Anna told me she had lived intermittently for some time at Taliesin, Frank Lloyd Wright's school of architecture in Spring Green, Wisconsin. Wright had married one of Gurdjieff's émigré students, a member of his core dance troupe which toured American cities and performed at Carnegie Hall in 1924. Olgivanna helped Wright run his school throughout his life and thereafter, until her own death in 1984.

Anna once expressed her admiration of Wright's school, which in those days was not unlike Gurdjieff's Institute in France, especially with regard to the role of practical work in all-round human development. In 1932, Wright opened the architectural program at Taliesin to accept apprentices in residence. Their training included work in the kitchen and gardens, the maintaining of the house and grounds, and movements classes taught by Olgivanna and by their daughter, Iovanna. The doors of Taliesin were open to the retinue—Jeanne de Salzmann, Thomas and Olga de Hartmann, and C.S. Nott—the latter having recorded his long stay with the Wrights in a book, *Journey through this World.*

"Now that was a center for Work!" Anna told me. Her eyes quickened with excitement. "You might think the pace of work here is demanding; at Taliesin, we were pushed to the limits. On weekends when guests would join us for a banquet, we would be working hard in the gardens, our clothes and ourselves covered in mud and clay, or Mrs. Wright holding us up in a meeting, until thirty minutes before supper. In that time we returned our tools, showered, dressed in formal attire, make-up and hair just right, to serve the guests or join them at the tables with grace and composure."

The origins of Gurdjieff's knowledge are a patchwork of second-hand assertions. Typical of this state of affairs, it was the recollections of a ten-year-old, Slovak-American girl that provided Bennett with his best clues on the lineage of Gurdjieff's principal training technique.

When Anna left Sherborne at the end of the second year, Michael Sutton replaced her.

MICHAEL'S MOVEMENTS CLASSES were famous. "Mick made you want to work, as if there is no tomorrow," was a common refrain. His infectious enthusiasm, the magical realism of his perception, cast a net over everyone within range. He would hold court for hours.

Michael was a savory concoction of extremes, and Bennett, an instinctive cook, was seasoning the pot when he brought Michael aboard. After Bennett died, Michael, who depended on him, went through a period which left later students remembering him for his seductions and drinking, his month-long withdrawals into his room.

Michael and I had a number of marathon carousals in India. He was no undermining influence; I was a full member of the club. He was, in fact, my lifeline. As in life itself, there are no hard rules for work; every one of us is a theater of possibilities. Michael took on the role of my elder and wiser brother.

Of his struggle to contain his phenomenal energy, Michael said, "I'm too leaky." He was diagnosed as having overactive adrenal glands. He told me that he refused treatment against the advice of doctors, opting for a shorter but livelier existence. Bennett helped him understand his energy and his talents and dispose them constructively. Michael's natural element was other people, who drew around him like schools of fish around the salmon king.

"I think the boy has philosophy," his wonderfully eccentric father once said over a pint of Worthington's Ale. Bennett, his spiritual father, put it to him this way: "You have 'third force': how you use it is now your responsibility." Bhante, too, said as much some years later: "Michael is a man of understanding; he could make a very good teacher."

Michael repeated a saying from Coombe, about the different fates people have in relation to the work: "make, bear, take, care." There are those who make work, those who must bear it, those who take from it, and those who care for it. Michael was the caretaker.

The moment I heard of his death, I felt the world's light dim. Some people say he threw his life away, but I always think of him as a fulfillment, and I was one of those who was increased.

This is brought back to me by Laurence Sutton: she met Michael on one of the Sherborne courses, and later they married. Recently she began writing about their life together:

> Paris, December 13, 1996
>
> Dear Allen,
>
> ... I often felt I should write my experiences of seven years with Michael. ... Michael wrote a proper diary, mainly about his life before he met Mr. Bennett. He talks about his different jobs, his friends, and the life in Kingston-upon-Thames, in the sixties. He describes all this brilliantly, and with high humor. ... George Cornelius begged Michael to continue. But Michael threw his diary across the room, saying it was only doodles to quiet his mind, and anyway that he was not a writer.
>
> ... We were in the Parisian Metro, and the crowd looked very gloomy, Michael thought. He didn't like that. He gave me a sigh and stood up in the middle of the train car. After a pause, a deep breath, he gave a heavy but kind look to everyone and said: I am not asking you for any money, neither for a restaurant ticket, nor for a job. All I am asking you for is A LITTLE SMILE!" No one had expected that (being used to other demands). Soon, people started to smile; some very frankly, others more shyly. But still there were a few that remained hostile, so Michael insisted again: "A lit-tle smi-le." Soon everybody smiled, except one lady stuck in her corner. So Michael went up to her and gently put his hand under her chin. Everybody laughed, and she finally broke out in laughter. The train stopped, and Michael said to me, "Come on, let's try next train!".

A friend of ours had become very Catholic, to the point of superstition. He always tried in a pushy way to have us come with him to all kinds of services at the church, mostly because he didn't want to go alone. We did join him several times, but this time we wouldn't; but he insisted so much and became so unbearable that Michael said, "O.K., we come with you, but wait, I go next door to get dressed properly." ... we see Michael dressed up like an Arab of Mecca, with the 'agal' (black circle) around his head, the white scarf, tunic, everything.

"You can't go like that!" screamed the friend, "Especially since I like to be in the front row." But this time it was Michael insisting: "Yes, yes! We have to go. We are going to miss the beginning." And he pushed him out of the flat and ran down the street to Notre Dame (the Old Bitch-as Michael used to call her affectionately). We attended the service in the front row, with our remorseful friend. He never asked us to join him again.

We met a young lady at a work week-end where Michael held a seminar. This young woman must have been impressed because, not one week after we got back to Paris, she knocked at our door, alone. She claimed she saw something that week-end that she had to continue here, in Paris, that it was urgent, more important than staying with her husband and children ... and could we put her up for a while. We let her stay overnight. The next morning her wish to stay with us was even stronger, and sighed, 'to Work!' Michael looked at her very seriously and told her, 'You have in your purse a very special cigarette holder, in chiseled silver.' At this point she blushed. 'Would you give it to me?' She had a frightened look and didn't answer. Michael repeated the question, which she tried to ignore, but began slowly gathering her things, then stood up. Michael gently took her to the door. She stood before us and said, "I must go. Goodbye."

Two years after Michael died, she came to me to ask if she could bury her cigarette holder in, or on, or next to Michael's grave. In spite of my arguments, she did it.

Michael's favorite subject remained, above all, food. Our very small kitchen had everything he needed to make a banquet. When people, friends, visitors would ask heavy questions, Michael had two "remedies": take them to the pub, and cook them a meal. He was the same with the plants and the animals. It was difficult to have animals in a small Parisian flat. But he managed to grow vegetables and exotic flowers on the one-meter square balcony and a tree in the main room that reached to the ceiling. Another dare was to build a chicken house on the roof of the very Parisian building where I live. He had to climb a ladder to reach the roof and feed them. There, he had an overall view of Paris at his feet, Notre Dame on his right, the Sacre Coeur of Montmartre in front of him, the Church of St. Germaine des Prés on his left, and further, the Dome of the Invalides and the Eiffel Tower. He felt like the King of Paris feeding his flock. But the ducks and chickens grew up. A duck fell six floors through the glass roof of the concierge and splashed right in the basin of water while the man was shaving himself. Even though he was not supposed to know where it came from (the "contract" between us was that nobody should know, as it was strictly forbidden), the concierge guessed who was the author, and within minutes a big bang on our door … and the man, holding the dead duck by the neck, just said, "Here is your duck!" Michael cooked canard á l'orange, a famous French recipe, and brought the concierge a big dish with a thigh of the duck. …

Hospital stories are not to be laughed about, but Michael still managed to make me laugh and amuse everybody. He had very much the soul of a clown.

When he talked about himself, it was a question of life and death. Once, after being in a hospital for five weeks, the doctors decided to keep him one more week. Michael got so upset that he summoned the whole medical body (le Corps Medical), that is, the big Professor, the main doctor and the nurses' boss, to come to his room, as he had something very important to tell them. Hard to believe, they all came. And this is what he told them: "You may think you have managed to cure my body, but you are killing my soul! And for this reason I want to leave this hospital now, and I want you to deliver to me an exit permit NOW!" He got it and left the same day.

He was a man of service. The others first. His greatest pleasure was to make people happy, at the cost of his own reputation. In that sense, he was a real Malamati.* But wherever he saw indulgence, conceit, selfishness, useless authoritarianism, he would become ruthless with such people. Very often, people that Michael helped in some crucial time of their life, all reported him as the compassionate one. Bennett did tell him once that he was the Compassionate Idiot.

So, I finish here. I could go on and on, and it could take the size of a book.

Affectionately, Laurence

* Malamati means, literally, one who follows "the path of blame."

CHAPTER ~ THIRTEEN

ONE MORNING I met Bennett at a stair landing. He stopped me and said, "I have just met your Bikhu." He was smiling broadly into my face. My mind went blank until Bhante's image entered it. Bennett had just returned from India and a three-day conference, convened by Sri Aurobindo, for spiritual leaders and teachers from around the globe to exchange their perceptions on the current resurgence of spiritual interests in the West.

"Bhante?" I dumbly asked.

"Michael gave me the address in Mehrauli. We got on very well, and he has agreed to come visit us." He was visibly pleased and impressed by the Monk. I was impressed with Bennett's ability to interest Bhante (who thought most gurus were hustlers) and others of his peerage in his experimental school. But before I could speak, Bennett spied someone else he wished to speak to and was off down the hall.

Bhante did come, the following year, and for every year thereafter, holding a month-long meditation seminar, with lessons in chromotherapeutic healing and health maintenance. It was a new phase in Bhante's ever-widening circle of contacts and friendships. His grandson On (Konthal Cheng) left India to attend the third year course.

Not having formerly trained with Bhante, I am not well equipped to describe his courses. I did have a ten-day retreat with him in California, eighteen years ago, where I met my wife, Betty. But I do remember him telling me back in Mehrauli something of his earlier years:

"I became a monk because my life of privilege had gotten me into difficulties which I could not get out of. So I took the traditional vow for one year to live as a begging monk, like young men do to complete their education, before they get a job, have family. And, do you know?—when we went to beg food, I always came back to the temple with the most food in my bowl. Why? because people love to give to me! (laughs) This one and that one look at me like I am a great monk, most sincere and wise looking. This embarrass me, because I did not know anything about Buddhism. What I knew of religion, no thinking man could take seriously.

"So, I began to read the Buddha's teaching, so that I would know what prayer to say when they ask blessing, or speak to them in the way they would expect me to. And to tell you the truth, the more I read, the more I understood about questions which had bothered me all my life. I became very serious in my study of the Buddha's teachings. I became sure that I must follow his way.

"But already there was a problem, because everyone I knew before continued to laugh and joke with me and treat me like I was the same person."

BHANTE'S NAME HAD been Bel Long, first native Cambodian appointed a district judge an later, governor of a province under the French regime. He spoke many languages. Smart, educated, bon vivant: mistresses, Paris suits, nice cars, the best whiskey. His story continues:

"I realized I would have to leave Cambodia and everything connected with my past life. I left a wife and a daughter behind. I went first to Burma and lived in the jungle with other monks. I went to other teachers, in Thailand. Eventually I needed to go to the birthland of the Buddha, and I made my way there after more wandering. My family knew nothing of me for thirty years."

Mick and I watched him at his mission, putting colored bottles out to stand in the sunlight for days, then bagging them off to his secret larder. He dispensed the most simple and competent medical treatment around. I saw people with hepatitis, a rather common but dangerous illness to get in India, recovering after a few days of rest with nothing but teaspoons of water from these bottles, eating what he prepared for them and basking under his colored lamps. He even cured one traveller diagnosed with rabies, saying afterwards that it was good that the patient came to him before the illness was far advanced. "Harder to cure", he said.

Some doctors from Georgetown were determined to make an extensive study of his color therapies and the results on patients over time. This would be invaluable, if they could get him to stay in one place for more than three months at a time.

In 1978, Betty and I were married by Bhante, and we later opened our house to him at his request. Bhante arrived in a Volkswagen bus with three long-haired men in their twenties. Two of them were being treated for something. One of them, Michael, was really sick, gray of skin, forebodingly weak. Bhante said nothing, as if not giving an illness the power of a name, but stayed close to him in our house for six weeks until they all were off with him on the next leg of his journey.

A year later I was tapped on the shoulder by Michael, all aglow and bright-eyed. He was enrolled in the American transplant of the Sherborne course, at Claymont Court in West Virginia.* For our hospitality, Michael expressed his gratitude sincerely. I ventured to ask what had been the nature of his illness. "Leukemia," he said, eyebrows arching incredulously. His doctors declared a total remission of symptoms. Only time will tell if it lasts. He was sure he had been given back his life.

BHANTE HAS RECEIVED his fair share of fame, in many countries including this

* The Claymont School for Continuous Education was active from 1974 until 1984.

one. The following appeared in syndicated newspapers, May 12, 1989:

> MONK RESTORES BIT OF PEACE TO STOCKTON,
> by Jane Gross, New York Times News Service
>
> STOCKTON–There were ghosts in the playground of the Cleveland Elementary School here, and fear in the hearts of Cambodian parents and their children, until the Venerable Dharmawara Mahathera came several months ago to offer a blessing.
>
> Chanting the Buddhist scripture and sprinkling holy water on the spots where five children were gunned down by a deranged drifter last January, the 100-year-old monk restored a measure of peace and comfort to a refugee community that had come to depend upon him.
>
> "We are going to take away the evil action of an evil man," said the monk, known as Bhante. "We are going to send the good spirit to those who lost their lives and purify this school, so the children can come to study again."
>
> The monk had come to this agricultural city ten years ago ... sophisticated and well traveled, a lawyer and a judge before he turned to religion, a friend and spiritual adviser to heads of state. He would ease the transition of his countrymen from the killing fields and the murderous Khmer Rouge to a new and mysterious home in central California.
>
> "I had known this country well enough to help them adapt themselves to the way of life and the thinking," Bhante said, his fluent English slowed by long, considered pauses.
>
> Until the terrible day when Patrick Purdy sprayed the schoolyard with gunfire, killing four Cambodian children and one Vietnamese, Bhante's spiritual tasks had been more mundane, but still considerable.
>
> He had welcomed the newest refugees to his makeshift Buddhist temple, a ramshackle wood frame house at the edge of town with sandals heaped on the front steps, a pagoda in the yard and an altar, tiered like a wedding cake, in the living room.
>
> For those with no place to live and nothing to eat, he provided temporary bed and board. For the rest, he remained the source of blessings, delivered in the ancient Pali language, that asked the end of sickness, suffering and fear.
>
> Stockton has 30,000 Southeast Asian refugees among its 189,000 residents, and 11,000 are Cambodians. ... "This country," he said, "has given them everything ... Mostly they are sick people, because of the shock of their lives, the wars upon wars, the violence and killing and destruction ... It is my view that anybody who comes here must respect this country and feel it is their own. ... To tell you frankly, wherever I am I consider that place my own. ... Now do you know I am citizen? That is because I do not want to be half—half here and half somewhere."

IN HIS ONE-HUNDRED and ninth year, he continues to move about the world like a droplet of mercury. His reputation continues to renew in new circles. Recently he was the guest of Bangkok society, a connection he forged not long ago when attending a conference of healers where a venerable old sage fell desperately, and mysteriously, ill. To everyone's relief and awe, the frail man recovered through Bhante's calm ministrations. I heard that Bhante was offered a comfortable permanent residence in Thailand, which would suit any man of his age and rank. He went (then retired) to Stockton, where his glamourless Buddhist temple welcomes and serves the needs of the Cambodian survivors who come to his door.

CHAPTER ~ FOURTEEN

THERE WERE SEVERAL other specialists and helpers that would come to Sherborne at Mr. Bennett's urging.

Anthony Blake came several times that first year: sometimes to conduct classes, at other times simply to participate in the work and mix with the students. Bennett pressed him to become involved with the program, increasingly so as the courses progressed. He eventually became a resident, ostensibly enrolled as another student, but sharing with Bennett the teaching of ideas from *The Dramatic Universe* and work ideas in general. When Bennett died of a stroke, in the middle of the fourth year, Blake, Elizabeth Bennett, Michael Sutton and a few other staff members who stayed on to see the year through, agreed to preside over the fifth and final Sherborne course, with Blake as senior lecturer. He has authored some interesting small works and an ambitious, larger book which, I venture, will be the codex of its subject: *The Intelligent Enneagram.*★

His reputation had a habit of preceding him, thanks in part to Bennett's letting it be known that "Tony understands *The Dramatic Universe* better than I do." This off-hand compliment doubtless served Bennett's agenda; it also placed expectations in the minds of most everyone Tony would meet at Coombe. But one need not be cued beforehand to recognize his unusual intelligence, of a kind not so much absorbed in thought, as in the preoccupation with how the mind reads its own experience, and how we connect with each other's experience through acts of communication.

His work with us was completely action-oriented. We usually assembled into the lower library, an ample room free of furniture, and spent more time on our feet than in sitting. There he staged an unpredictable mix of mimes, group interactions, experiments in memory, perception of time and space, and so on. I do not recall him stating goals to us, but the exercises spoke for themselves. These simple theater pieces exploded time and turned space upside down. What we should expect to see or take away from the experience was not always stated.

I remember one of these improvisations vividly. It was deceptively simple: execute a series of spontaneous actions—such as standing up, walking across the room, opening a book, looking out the window, replacing the book, and so on. While executing each new action, we were to report aloud our previous action,

★ Shambhala. *The Intelligent Enneagram,* 1998.

but in present tense, as if we were still in the middle of performing it; that is, while walking across the room I say, "I am standing up"; then, while opening a book I say, "I am walking across the room." The room became a ward of inmates muttering to themselves, transformed into a scene from Marat-Sade.

The exercise simultaneously engaged my memory, coordination, and receptivity. I had to announce to the room what I had just finished doing, as if I were in the middle of doing it; at the same time I had to be executing my next action; at the same time I had to be seeking another action to follow. I experienced a wholly new sensation of the present. I habitually pictured the present as a moving point along a line. Now this point appeared to be a staging area which could contract or expand in three directions: the conditions of the past, the potentialities of the future, and consciousness insinuating itself upon the present. The impression defies words but can be evoked by repeating the experiment.

While these work sessions appeared to be without order, I sensed we were penetrating deeper and deeper into unspecified territory. Hours or days afterward, a fragment would come back to trigger an understanding.

What was most refreshing about working with Tony Blake was his complete openness to exploration. There was nothing rigid or doctrinaire in his make-up, nor in his approach to "work ideas." He visibly recoiled at the expression, as claque-language. He thrived in informal and relaxed conversation, which ranged over the length and breadth of popular culture, from Mickey Spillaine to Tarkovsky. I once mused that someone ought to make a film of *The Dramatic Universe.* Tony's eyes rolled back in his head: "My God, yes!" He was off on a comet of possibilities.

ABOUT TWO MONTHS into the course, John Allen arrived, in unlaced combat boots and army fatigues, with a squad of young adults who by appearance blended with the rest of us. They observed all the social graces after hours, but they were heavy business in the drama sessions. John Allen was pushing forty, confident and serious as cancer.

The first morning after their unannounced arrival, Bennett introduced them and left us in their hands for the next two weeks. The ninety of us met in the ballroom and formed into a ring. An angry young virago sprang into the circle and proceeded to scourge us with profanity, pacing about like a caged bobcat. She spat a couple of times and tripped over a cuss-word, which softened the shock, but she threw everything into it and succeeded in offending enough of us to justify her effort.

We spent the next half-hour contorting our face muscles into grimaces of loathing, laughter, mania, grief, horror, and clown expressions. We imitated as she rolled her outstretched arms around in their shoulder sockets, twisting them front to back, back to front, to the limits of their construction, and well beyond the time when agony began to set in. We twisted our hands likewise, with fingers splayed as if they were being extracted. All the while we continued contorting our faces, stretching jaws, being ugly.

John Allen stepped in after warm-up sessions like these and ran us through a gauntlet of skits and exercises which I found very interesting. I had experience with expressing emotion in encounter groups; so the theatrical confrontations did not challenge me in the same way as they did Moshe, a dignified, rather guarded individual. Moshe later declared that this theatrical work-out was a self-revelation. John Allen's people had broken through his stone-like composure until there was no place to hide. "If I get nothing else from this year," he said, "I will consider it time well spent."

Elizabeth Bennett, as I said, found the whole affair inappropriate; she held her tongue and made herself scarce.

In the last week we were divided into three troupes, with Allen directing each one in a day-long improvisation. My group performed something called "Famine in the Midst of Plenty." The structure was that of a miracle play, the action surrounding a single character, with everyone else assuming a myriad of stand-in roles—incidental, probing roles which Allen deduced from the play's progress. The student who volunteered for the first role of the day found that he had just signed on for an unbroken six-hour performance. An Afro-haired rock musician, this student would play the existential Traveler, in all of his emotional and spiritual aspects, his light and dark sides, under the conditions imposed upon him by society, culture, class, religion, sexuality, dependencies, addictions, aspirations. The Traveler eventually finds himself standing before The Most Holy Sun Absolute, Gurdjieff's name for the place of God's existence. Tony Blake, who had stuck his head through the door to view the proceedings, was immediately drafted for the Creator's cameo appearance.

John clearly had the confidence and loyalty of his troupe, who lived with him in a communal environment. His Theater of All Possibilities was one in a line of ambitious ventures. They built a fully-rigged and powered ferro-cement Chinese junk, sailed the oceans, stopping off to work a ranch in Australia. They designed, built and operated a hotel in downtown Kathmandu; operated and provided avant garde entertainment for a theater restaurant in Fort Worth.

Two decades later, one of his projects culminated in notoriety of sorts—Biosphere II, in Oracle, Arizona. It was John Allen's idea and Sam Bass' money. Bass was scion of a Texas dynasty and joined Allen's band after they returned from Sherborne. I recognized a few of them when I met Biosphere II management at a party years later. I could remember when we were all thrown together in that big house in the Cotswolds.

One day a curious thing happened, which marked the degree to which the Sherborne residents had become mutually-supportive of their efforts.

Everyone, including Allen's people, were to participate in a movements session one morning. We lined ourselves up in files spanning the ballroom, Bennett facing from the alcove. Somewhere in the middle of the session he held out his arms sideways, smiling cheerfully. Everyone did the same. After five or six minutes people were showing strain; I could see everyone from my position against the wall at one end of the room.

Bennett began to walk in place. This somewhat distracted us from our complaining arms. This went on for more long minutes, after which he stopped, his arms still out. He turned round again to face us, smiling cheerfully. Someone finally succumbed to the pain and dropped their arms. Then another, a third. Two or three more dropped their arms, but the rest held on for another long minute until Bennett let his arms down slowly, his shoulders and face muscles completely relaxed, as if he had not been in his body at all. (Michael told me, cracking up, that Bennett visualized angels holding his arms up.)

I noted that all but one person who dropped their arms were members of John Allen's retinue. There it was in spades: Sherborne people, myself included, had become, well, a group. We were drawing from a common well, an octane higher than that which anyone could produce alone, even Bennett himself. We together were going one better than our limits, day after day, week after week.

One of John's troupe enrolled in Sherborne the following year.

AN OLD TURKISH man paid us a prolonged visit. His name was Hasan Sushud, Hasan Bey, or Hasan—accent on the second syllable. I saw him four or five times personally and drove him to Cheltenham for the day. We saw him evenings, when he joined us and Bennett, who took the *muezzin's* part in the *namaz,* the muslim ritual prayer which we observed at end of day. Hasan stayed a distance behind the tall *muezzin* and to one side, like an altar boy. I have not seen a more expressive gesture of humility as Hasan's genuflection, as if to occupy as little of God's space as possible.

Little more than five feet in height in his ancient, double-breasted suit, the lines of Hasan's face were that of an old cleric or priest. Crinkled gray hair made a laurel wreath around his pate. The swoon-like gaze seemed to be taking in a good deal more around him than I could see myself. His fasts exceeded his periods for eating. He practiced a perpetual breathing exercise, which Bennett introduced us to some time before his arrival.

With a dozen students, I watched him from my place on the floor of his guest room as he spoke a few opening nonsequiturs to us. He looked, not only at us, but around and above us. I palpably felt other presences in the room. I looked over my shoulder, as if to see something, and I did. The high-ceilinged room was swimming in a resonating pale light, the texture and color of yellowed lace. Transparent entities skittered through it, like a school of ghost-glass catfish in a tank. I had the distinct impression of seeing angels! I turned my face back to Hasan, who seemed to have me in his peripheral sight. I swear he knew perfectly well what I was experiencing. My heart would like to have stopped, but the opposite happened; I suddenly became relaxed.

Hasan's presence was a complexity. He appeared frail, bearing pain somewhere within him, yet he remained soaring and free. My first impression of him was of a spirit who looks back at us from the other side of a veil, as we gape back at him, dumbstruck.

"The body is not material." He was sitting on the end of his bed, cross-legged, a scarf wrapped around his neck, because he was suffering from a cold. He was speaking only when inspired to do so. No one made a move during the silences. No one prepared us for this, whatever it was. I asked no questions, as I remember, but listened and watched attentively. I remember him repeating again after a pause, so that we would remember, "It's the body that's not material!"

Something inside took flight when I heard it. The idea was of course preposterous, yet absolutely right. My awareness had shifted to my sensation body, and what he said became more tangible. My body had become less dense, light as a silk shirt.

Hasan was here ostensibly to teach breathing and fasting and oversee its effects on these new initiates. I believe there was something more fundamental in his coming. His friend and spiritual protégé, Mr. Bennett, arranged for us to feel Hasan's presence, as one who has "pierced the veil." Hasan confided to Bennett that we were rather bluff, without much of life's honing; he would pray to God to send him better candidates next year. As he met with more of us, however, his opinion changed, or so he said, and he praised each successive group who met with him for being so much more promising than those who came before. He probably was playing with us a little, but nonetheless delivered it with a straight face.

He was able to say to Mr. Bennett, upon his leaving, that he had lost his reservations and now thought the school was exceptionally well-suited to modern conditions, especially for the West.

Hasan's mode of living was a never-ending *Ramadan,* a turning toward God, of which his two practices of conscious breathing and fasting were the outer manifestation. They were the divine feast. He told us that his wife and doctor pester him to eat more regularly and take better care of himself.

NOT ALL FOUND Sherborne students amenable. When Idries Shah came to pay his respects, he observed us somewhat differently. For us he was a visiting celebrity and a flesh and blood connection with the Inner Circle of Humanity, as it were.

"I am like the man who has painted himself into a corner," were his opening words, seated before us in Bennett's red velvet butler's chair in the lower library. He chain-smoked Benson and Hedges, glibly careening from one subject to another. Very intelligent, very quick, Bennett warned us that a good deal of nonsense could be expected; but listen attentively, and something comes through. That was all.

The floor was not open to questions until the end of his talk. We paused for high tea in the guest's honor. Shah found himself cornered by a half-dozen gawkers, one or two trying ham-handedly to draw him out. At end of day I saw Bennett and Shah walking slowly on the cinder path, heads down, after which

Shah left without ceremony. Bennett repeated Shah's impression of us the next day. He felt like he was being circled by sharks. "In the East," Bennett continued kindly, but saddened, "people are more sensitive to one another, and they observe a hundred courtesies that never occur to us westerners. Who can really say if this is superior to the crudeness with which we treated Shah?"

Bennett had repeated enough of Shah's assessment to deflate any rising estimation of ourselves. I understand that Shah never returned to Sherborne.I have just recently, however, received a photograph from Mr. Gerald Green, the former mayor of Northleach, the town nearest to Sherborne. The photo shows a carved stone column flanked by yew hedges, above which Sherborne's church steeple points skyward. Surmounting the tall column is a turban-capped urn garlanded in stone roses. Gerald Green writes on the back of the picture: "The stone ornament that Idries Shah gave to Mr. Bennett after giving talks at Sherborne House."

CHAPTER ~ FIFTEEN

"I CAN SERVE as an example for you," Bennett said early in the course, "as one who has experienced this work. But this can only be a phase of necessary dependency, beyond which our work must come from ourselves. That is my great hope for you, before you leave here."

I contrasted this with statements he made in the lecture he gave in London, attended by a bus-load of us. The subject was the International Academy for Continuous Education, launched at Sherborne village some months before. A gentleman in the audience raised his hand, stood up and projected his question with the confidence of one who already knows the answer: "How much of the school's functioning depends upon your being its leader?"

"There is no leader," Bennett dissembled. "The school can be run by any number of specialists. I bring my experience to it, but I am not indispensable. In this work there are no gurus."

"How many do you have as staff in the Academy, and what is their contribution?" the man persisted, still standing. "There are several others, all of whom have experience," Bennett replied, still not meeting the issue head on. Sitting in the audience, I had to admit that no one but Bennett himself, through his colossal sense of mission, could generate such determination in ordinary people. Having set the question up for everyone to consider and seeing that Bennett would not concede the point, the gentleman sat down. For Bennett to answer with candor would have been premature; he had not as yet spoken a word of the further developments he contemplated for the alumni. He intended for the administration of the basic course to be put in the hands of graduates as soon as possible. He also foresaw the school itself as the first stage of a larger social experiment.

He spoke about the possibility, and need, for a form of human community which recognizes the authority of wisdom and presence of being. This society recognizes the existence of the wise and takes their example; it would assist in the arising of all beings who stand on lower rungs of their development. It is a kinetic situation, but with the integrity of a self-sustaining structure.

I am still not convinced that Bennett was utopian. He had few illusions about his people. He knew they were strong together and weak apart. He knew they could consciously cooperate toward a common aim. They needed to be given something to do.

There is a condition which people cannot get around, that one learns something by teaching it to someone else. We had to become teachers. (Just once would probably suffice your need.) It would become part of a person's life, no matter how brief.

When we leave here, he predicted, we will have to find our own way, which for many of us will be to seek professions and skills for livelihood—to become good householders. But there is a need for a psychokinetic society—a social arrangement founded on the perfecting of its individual members—as distinguished from stagnating, psychostatic communities, where the possibilities for man's development are circumscribed by changing social conventions, the mismanagement of information, and consumerism.

Such a society could begin with a gathering of a trained group of "specialists." In that situation, the question of the need for a strong and wise leader, such as John Bennett, would be proven in real situations.

We would learn soon enough to live without him, and learn something about who we were. As soon, in fact, as the opening of the American Society for Continuous Education, Inc., founded on the newly-purchased rural acreage of Claymont Court, near Charles Town, West Virginia, in 1976.

Bennett would have presided over both of these two centers for continuous education at once. I am sure he could have done it, but it was not in his lot. He died of a stroke during the fourth Sherborne course, only months before several Sherborne graduates and their families, with Pierre Elliot, decided to open the doors according to plan.

THROUGHOUT THE COURSE Bennett communicated nothing but optimism for us, but he frequently doused it with frank appraisals of our immediate prospects: very few of us, maybe one or two, will make such-and-such important step while we are here. The rest of us would pass on into the world outside, in conditions much less amenable.

"Maybe I get more out of this than any one of you," he said to us about three months before the course ended. It was not how he would have spent the last of his years. His life in retrospect, however, had been a preparation for it. "We come here," he said, "because we have seen that we are in need of something that life itself cannot provide to us. An opportunity has come for another purpose, which we may not even comprehend. But anyone can see that the world is in great trouble and seems unable to get out of it by itself. It cannot be cured by a miracle, or religious revival, much less a political movement. The world will be helped only by growing numbers of people trying to awaken." We find in this idea a force for our own work. That is why, in morning exercise, we turn our attention to the presence of all of us together in the room. We are building a reservoir that we can draw upon after we leave here."

The issue of group work came up more in the last months. Few of us would make good groupies, I thought. After all, Sherborne was not a recruiting station.

Some years later, Manfred Blum published some private editions of fragments from Bennett's talks. One of these slender anthologies records him asking:

"Is it a form of weakness that people need each other? Is it a form of weakness that my thumb needs my fingers to pick something up? It is a very poor kind of thumb which cannot hold a knife by itself—we do not say that. It is not weakness at all. We belong to one another in the way that fingers and thumbs do. We cannot do without each other. About this Gurdjieff used to say that the first truth revealed to man by God is that one hand washes the other."

CHAPTER ~ SIXTEEN

FOR BENNETT, the "Purgatory" chapter of *Beelzebub's Tales* was scripture for our time. That picture of the world he investigates by geometry in *The Dramatic Universe,* Vol. 1. Not once did I hear him explain any of it in his talks. He did talk on cosmology, more and more as time drew on.

"There are three views on the nature of this world," a student records him saying. "One is that it is a place of constant struggle between good and evil. The second view is that it is a world of Maya, without significance, and the only real goal is to escape from the illusion. The third is that the world is evolving. It is hard to reconcile these three views of the world; but I will say that the one that is right for our time is this third view. What we do in this world is significant and important and, at the same time insignificant and illusory. We must keep both of these truths in mind."

For understanding the universal situation, he went back time and again to "Holy Planet Purgatory" and the tale of how our Maker-Creator Endlessness once had to confront the merciless flow of time.

Time, Beelzebub explains, would eventually wear down everything by exhausting all the possibilities flowing from His place of existence. Time is an independent agent, more a consequence of the given than of itself an absolute. Its entropic action had to be compensated for. Enter the "second creation."

The Maker-Creator resolved to introduce into the laws of world creation and maintenance, structural discontinuities—gaps in the fabric where incursions are made possible and essential. Everything will tend to drift off-course, unless revivified at critical points by outside influences. A world doomed to heat-death is given the capability of self-renewal. This world is more process than thing, where winning and losing is the given and there are few guarantees. The Megalocosmos is now hazardous, dramatic and intrinsically interesting.

From this second creation, or readjustment of the laws of the first creation, came a growing metamorphosis of forms and co-dependencies, among which was the notable arising of independent intelligences. A new possibility enters the picture, of beings who can understand where they are in the Megalocosmos. With that understanding, the newly arisen localized intelligences could reduce the total burden placed upon Our Creator Endlessness.

Thus Man enters the picture, as an essence class of beings capable of playing a creative role in the evolution of the world. Presto, the meaning of life.

And just as our "Unique-Burden-Bearing-Endlessness" had to bring intelligence to bear in order to renew the place of His existence, Bennett interpreted for us, we must do the same in order to renew the place of our existence. That is to say: renew our world, our bodies, our higher being bodies, and our soul.

Developing a higher being body was, strange to say, the most tangible part of the Sherborne curriculum. Bennett likened the process to a ten-month pregnancy, where a ghostly interior can begin to coalesce, take shape:

"The 'body kezdjan' (Turkish *kez*, vessel, and Persian *jan*, soul) is a measure of our interior substantiality. This second body is no more than a ghost or shadow. It exists in the world of energies, which includes the world of spirits, thought-forms, and dreams. It is the *alam-i-arvah* of the Sufis.

"The lower extremities of this world overlap the 'material' world. This is the level that spiritualism is concerned with. It is a state of existence which is only a dreamlike replica of physical existence, but without the physical world to set its limits.

"To be in that world can be a pleasant experience, as it can be a very terrifying experience, because we can meet with things in that world that are the thought-forms of one's own life. All this is more or less available to investigation, and people have attached a great deal of importance to it because they believe it proves survival beyond death. But what kind of survival and what value it has, they don't ask."

THEN HE TOLD THIS STORY: "I knew a man who asked that question very seriously. He came to me about fifteen or twenty years ago—he was one of the foremost leaders in the spiritual movement in England and was regarded as a great authority in mediums and had experiences of his own—and said, 'I have come to the conclusion that spiritualism only leads up to a certain point, and everything that matters is beyond that point and how one gets beyond that point. It is no longer of any interest to me that something survives death, because that kind of survival is not at all what I was looking for when I began this search.'"

When I heard this I thought, how odd, that I was now in a position to relate by experience to this idea of a second body, which can become more robust, more substantial, than the physical body. Bennett said it can develop intelligence, but without a will to regularly rouse this passive, second-being body out of its trance-like quasi-existence, it experiences no further growth. No continuous education.

Responding to the question, Does man have a soul?, Gurdjieff answered by saying that he does not. "But he has something which takes its place. It is like a cloud that travels in different parts of him, and wherever this cloud happens to be, there is his center of gravity. In the other parts of him where it is not, there is a feeling that nothing there matters. If it is in the head, everything in the head matters and the body and the feelings do not. Because it cannot be in all places at once, we have a division of centers within ourselves."

Bennett added, "The more organized the cloud becomes, the more conscious participation there is with the other world, the *alam-i arvah."*

We do not notice that we live in these two spheres of experience, first of all because we do not distinguish between images and genuine perceptions.

"We have entered a new phase of work, the mesoteric stage, which concentrates on the formation of our second body. Of course, no one should expect that the process can be completed in the little time we have together; but it is possible within this time to make a good beginning, so that this may continue to grow after you leave." Perhaps, he would add, very few of you will be able to take the step of entering upon this next phase of work.

The matter-of-factness, with which Bennett first declared this aim, struck me as a little crazy. Now I knew he had been speaking in concrete terms. I had palpable experience of a body within, still forming. This had to be, I thought, the opportunity of a lifetime.

Time was slipping by, just as it always does on the "outside"—that is, the world outside the Sherborne bubble. I could look over my own shoulder and find a trail of lost opportunities. I grieved to possess some of these passing minutes before they vanished forever.

I had filled a notebook with esoteric bits from the talks and lectures. I clustered these blocks of information and color coded them with page after page of diagrams. This replica of fruitful effort became more and more transparent as time drew on. My own observations and experiences went unrecorded, as if they had no validity. I could not find myself anywhere in my so-called record of the course. Around February I began to keep a proper journal.

I remembered Elizabeth Bennett warning us, "One day you will find yourself looking back on your time here, and it will be just as if it were all a dream." Even though I knew it had to be true, the thought suddenly terrified me. Already I saw my first months here as retreating memories. The novelty of the Sherborne course, this spiritual grand tour in the peaceful Cotswold countryside, began to look more like purgatory had just arrived.

CHAPTER ~ SEVENTEEN

BY FEBRUARY Everyone knew each other well enough to have nothing more to hide. Our personalities and our negative sides were public domain. There was a healthy air of mutual acceptance which got us through months of histrionics and personal crisis. Those who acted out their travails were a blessed relief for the rest of us who had no talent for manifesting. Disapproval and enmity between us was markedly absent, although I would venture to guess that we all had some favorite person to despise. One woman, to whom I was initially attracted, I would later find unbearable. The feeling was mutual. Negative sparks flew between us across the dining table. This unpleasant chemistry eventually spent itself, to our mutual relief. We became friends in the end.

I sensed that the harmony of the community could easily disintegrate without the watchful eyes of the Bennetts. Mr. Bennett met emotional explosion and general craziness with calm and astute perspective. Over decades he had overseen a multitude of off-the-wall situations, especially during the Subud days. By faith in providence and in his own powers, he helped turn personal crisis to benefit, for the sufferer and for the general good of his community. But Bennett would never traffic with sensationalism. He met frivolous displays of emotion or personality with cold disdain.

"I wish I could tell you otherwise, that the growth of our own being can happen without suffering. But that is not the case. All paths for forming a soul require from everyone a certain amount of suffering. This suffering is very small in comparison with the rewards. But it is not easy. And the further one goes, the harder it gets."

We comported ourselves with guileless candor, safe in the sphere of our common experience. The spectacle of interaction, between ourselves and people visiting our school, often appeared strange to me. The artifice of conversation, our incognizance of what was going on outside our community, served to remind me how it will be, how I will be, back in the Land of Men. That is, unless some big step is made before I am shown the door in August.

IN LATE SPRING while my group was arriving for movements, I found myself standing by the concert grand, looking into the cavity of strings and hammers. A twenty-year old American girl appeared from the rim of my vision and slid onto the bench. Her fingers spread above the keyboard, like a bird about to seize its prey. Her hands plunged and filled the room with the opening of a fearsome concerto, which got my attention right away—as much for its technical skill and inventiveness, as for its high drama. I liked it. It even managed to fit into the house's collected atmosphere.

Anna Durco hovered behind her, for once looking indecisive. The performance was so intensely charged that Anna silently allowed her to time her own exit—but be damn quick about it, she exuded. A suitable transition came soon enough. She quietly left the piano to take her place for movements. The room bristled.

The next day I asked her if she were the composer.

"It's called Kent State, and yes, I'm the composer." In one sitting, the day after the Ohio National Guardsmen opened fire on the students.

This surprise performance, however, was not just her debut, but a portent. From that day on she seemed to me to be out of her chrysalis, into a supercharged, gregarious state, which lasted for weeks and weeks. She buttonholed people or woke them in the dead of night to speak the truth of themselves to them. I had no trouble according respect for her elevated level of perception, in spite of the hysterical side to it. Highly gifted, melodramatic, uncaring about her personal appearance, she became for me emblematic of the state of the whole household. She fit in just fine.

One evening we assembled for meditation in the ballroom. Bennett sat cross-legged on the floor in his usual place—the English sheik on his cushion, women arrayed along the wall to his left, men on his right, facing each other. The young women sat in a simple chair to one side of Bennett, with bow and cello. She had acquired one at Bennett's behest, giving her the task to acquaint herself with the instrument, then extemporize one evening, unannounced, just before meditation. She calmly waited, centered. At the right instant after the silence settled in, she played a simple music which seemed to unify the entire room.

Nothing could have focused her mind more productively. I believed that Bennett was the (white) magician Gerald Wilde declared him to be. Better yet, a brilliant therapist. "Mr. B" had adroitly tossed her an anchor, without diminishing her high-flying energy. He could have done the safe thing and draw on the several options, such as counterbalancing exercises, available to him, which she would do if he asked, but he chose to interfere as little as possible.

He surely had this student in mind, when one evening he explained the meaning of a Sufi word, *jazba:* a spiritual condition that can be clarifying or delusional, or both. A Persian-English dictionary defines *jazba* as passion, rage, fury; strong desire, craving. A second dictionary leaves another impression—of charisma, ravishment, rapture, ecstasy, transport, bliss. A third simply cites ravishment, rapture.

The subject is impelled to express and act, without much regard for convention. Visions of the divine can be expected. The ecstatic often comes down with a crash.

Bennett's counsel was founded on assumptions differing from contemporary psychological thinking. We presently understand such behavior as manic episode, best treated straightaway with a course of medication, hoping to strike a psychosomatic balance. Bennett gave out that such states can be a gift. He described the state of *jazba* as our lower nature unable to bear the soaring flights of our higher nature.

His casual demeanor nevertheless communicated caution: learn to tread water, to separate, observe what is happening, don't over-value experiences you may have, and come to him when you need to. Some of us had been speaking privately with him regularly. The women of whom I speak had been meeting privately with Bennett from the beginning. He recognized her exceptional gifts.

After more long weeks, Laurie brought into the theme meeting gothic renderings of a number of interior episodes, climaxing with her standing speechless and alone, Hamlet-like, in a remote corridor of the house. Bennett listened with interest but said nothing for some time. Then, hesitatingly, looking for the right way to put it, he said that what she experienced was real and important, "but … too much literature." Laurie was visibly relieved, if for nothing else than by having articulated something of her experience, objectively and accurately. She began to calm down over the following days, as I remember.

I related to Laurie's experience, having gone through a somewhat similar experience myself. Not as noticeable or long lasting—about twelve days, my journal says. I did not, for instance, become prophetic.

My energy level went through the ceiling. Everything seemed to have been let free. *I* was free.

> April 9. Third day of feeling like I'm on speed.
>
> I saw myself dashing about, talking rapidly. The day was full of activity. Felt exhilarated and full of myself. Made peace with the house guest (who rubbed me the wrong way).
>
> Hasan Bey is here to teach us to fast. This morning in theme I wanted to really work with the fasting. Great hope for future. But during meditation, I saw myself getting back to my old ways—even planning to. This was terrifying, because no one around will stop me but myself. Right now something is happening in the School that is working on me, and I don't want to lose it.

I made an appointment to speak to Bennett. He asked me how long it had been going on. I told him a week or more; I was not precise. I told him I had great desire to make this count for me, not merely enjoy the experience. I wanted to work with it. I wanted …. Bennett just laughed and said, "Yes, it is like that." He opened his large hands and raised his eyes heavenward: "The heart longs to be swept up, to be made an angel's …." He added with a wink, "It will help to remember, later on, that an opposite reaction is also coming."

I remember the episode ending with an emotional plunge. I also remember watching it descend gradually over days. I have only my journal to give it any definition.

> April 12. Personality is glorifying itself over these last few days. I am picturing myself as "saintly." I managed to stop negative reactions in dining room, by changing posture. I try to eat consciously, but I also notice that I am trying to cover up, act humble, or look like I am concealing my efforts. Always attempting to look like something. Less speedy today, low on energy around five o'clock. Took bath, came away relaxed, good spirits.
>
> April 13. Identified with being "boss"—was bossy to planters and they snapped back. My spirits sank, and today has been lower key. Still, fasting did not make me as negative as it usually does. Experienced real pleasure working in the garden.
>
> April 14. Desire for cigarettes and intoxicants again. Personality displayed itself in movements today; couldn't stop it: the way my eyes moved around, making expressions, the clicking tongue, all of it for projecting a me that doesn't even exist. I made attempts to look at my "unfavorites" without animosity, with some success. I worked during gardening only with what I "like" to do.

The last stage of the course, individualized work, would be no better than our first-hand knowledge of ourselves. I thought I was seeing nothing but a thin veneer of myself, although I was wrong. I was seeing plenty, but I did not know how to evaluate my perceptions. So I recorded little about myself except my social reactions, marital strife, and cravings to medicate myself. I was having insights and experiences constantly!—all unrecorded. Where was all this material going after leaving short-term memory? Certainly not into my notebook.

I considered my lackluster participation in this crash course. Why, I had to ask, did I not desire to organize my work, make consistent efforts? Well, because of a lifetime of habits, gratifications, and mind sets that were not about to leave without a fight. Then came the April 21 entry [quoted in full on page 70] which records a return of a craving for stimulation, for pleasurable spending sprees of all available energy. I was plunging into anomy, with a conviction of helplessness, in spite of Bennett's high regard for negative states as our chief source of opportunities. I had already forgotten my spiritual elation of days ago:

> April 21. No hope to free myself from the pull of the world. ... The philosophy is beginning to alienate me. ...

There appears, however, evidence of understanding:

> Such skepticism is not producing anything, because it doesn't come from a wish for truth, but from hurt feelings, self pity, and disgust with having to go against my desires and hungers, and soon. This skepticism comes as a defense *against anything that places demands on me.*

There follows a five-week hiatus in my journal, where nothing was written until the evening after my first meeting with Hasan Bey, as I have described in an earlier chapter. I must have experienced a day of exceptional clarity following his curious exchange with us:

> May 29. Hasan Sushud says and emphasizes that the body is not material. Tonight in meditation I saw that I am seeking resolution of problems outside of me, and the only answers to them are worked out within. It is as if a magnet draws me outward, away from the inner world. But I saw for myself that it is real inside, but unreal, not even material, out there. But I know the strength of its pull. I wish therefore to remember what I now know, that reality and resolution are found within, and once a day I wish to enter there and make contact, after I leave here.
>
> These problems are illusions. How "I" am "offended by others," disappointed in my personality and the impressions I make—and fail to make—on others. All this is of the outside and will not be resolved. It all comes in through the sense organs of an immaterial body. All description. If I see this for myself, there is hope.

In telling stories of what happened to others during our ten months together, I run the risk of getting things quite wrong. Memories which have volunteered to come out have been written over by the passing of time. My memories are after-images containing splices of interactions in open and uncensored conditions.

I witnessed a number of future marriages in their germinal stage, and the same number of marriages coming apart. The whys and wherefores were not public knowledge or a matter for group discussion. But we can see a great deal about other people that they do not see themselves, by witnessing their ways of manifesting and reacting. Admitting that, it is equally true that we do not experience another person's existence. Although this may be possible—and Bennett certainly believed it so—we are too self-absorbed to enter into the existence of another for an instant.

After all these years of knowing better, I still fall under the spell that I am the object of everyone's attention; that deep down beneath it all, I am the center of existence! The hold that this trick of the mind has upon us is tenacious and for some people there is no respite. Everyone is watching me because I'm the one who's *really* here!—the object of endless fascination for all sentient beings right up to Mr. God Himself. This endemic self-regard is a world unto itself—a zombie-like world—the place where everyone puts in significant amounts of time. So much for an outside audience watching over us.

This is not to say that our day-to-day experience of others is more "objective" and the experience of ourselves more "subjective," or vice-versa. Both kinds of information are there. Bennett was good at dispelling pseudo-contradictions. In the different worlds we live in, he said, we learn different kinds of things.

"We actually care about what others think of us!" Bennett marveled, as if it were the most incredible aberration in the whole outlandish universe. "Even after seeing again and again how we are, how we live: men looking at women, women looking at men, people looking at food …" No nervous giggles from the room: in silence we felt the weight of his perplexity, the dreary monotones in people's lives.

THE SOMEWHAT HARDENED manner of Virgil Walker had undergone considerable change by mid-spring, since I had helped pull up rotted floor boards in the room assigned to him, his wife Sharon, and three children—Krishna, Kenny, and Diane. His first comment was droll: he was going to have trouble getting used to all the hippies. He told me he'd been a cop in the sixties, and the experience had a bad aftertaste. He got out of that business, not out of resentment, but because he was thriving on the excitement. He disliked what it was turning him into.

Bennett's first meeting with Virgil had in fact been a confrontation. Bennett's habit, when first sitting down with someone for a private chat, was to say a few words of no importance, then shut his eyes, wait for cacophony to settle, summon up his next words while sensing their mutual presence. "You're a violent man, aren't you?" Virgil answered in the only way he could in one word: "Yes."

As it turned out, Virgil and Sharon moved into the gate house on the private drive connecting to the highway. Virgil spent his off-hours getting the place livable. Sharon charmed the recluse artist, Gerald Wilde, out of his windowless lair to become her regular visitor. They cracked jokes in a private language while she hung out the family's laundry. Sharon was not enrolled on the course per se, but her participation in the community life was such that I was not aware of a special status. "I don't want you to come to the classes, except the morning exercise and the other house functions. You are one who will learn on your own," Bennett told her.

Virgil and I sat opposite each other one night at the pub. Students were crowding in and drowning the place with conversation and laughter. Virgil was remembering a side of himself he had forgotten after enduring his parents' divorce and escaping bespectacled nerdity by a path of aggressive survival skills. Conservative, libertarian, Mormon, a good cop, he was a promising painter. He was also color blind. During his days in law enforcement, he would park his patrol car on high roadsides around Flagstaff to paint the dawn on small, precut canvases he packed around, occasionally asking his partner what the color was on the end of his brush.

When Virgil seemed to have reached a stopping place in his story, I confided a recent episode: my nocturnal walk along the highway to Oxford only the week before, inspired by an evening of drinking under a full moon. I had walked all night till dawn, sixteen miles. When the sun broke dead center on the eastbound highway, the light seared my eyes and brain, and the dam of exhaustion burst, stopping me in my tracks. I crossed the road to hitch back to Sherborne House, returned to my room and slept for eighteen hours straight. I discovered that the soles of my shoes were worn through.

"So you do things like that, too." he said, in recognition. He then began speaking about himself in the present tense, a Virgil who was now forty pounds lighter, whose face had changed character. The commitments of his personal life, and to his religion, which sustained him, were unraveling with ominous finality. His energy level made it impossible to sleep; he hadn't for six nights running. A Mormon who never drank, Virgil was downing shots of whiskey to ballast himself. While he told this tale, I watched the knuckles of his thumbs drain white from pressing ever harder against the rim of his stout shot glass, until a little explosion went off in his hands. They were covered in blood. I went to the barman for a towel or bandage and wrapped his bleeding thumb up, after which we continued talking for another hour before we went back to the house.

Bennett took all our collective fretting in stride, convincing us that he knew what we were able to bear. He censured no one, other than by force of his example. He related to us in the only terms that interested him—our work. How we were at the moment, he served back to us straight, like a litmus test. There was no place to hide at Sherborne, certainly not behind the masks of custom and propriety. Our reactions and defenses mattered little to him; his interest was in the slow and least observed process of assimilation particular to each of us.

He foresaw we would need outside help, the kind of help that comes only when sincerely petitioned. For this he had recourse to a morning practice, which at one point I almost refused to perform.

"I wish," was associated with a place in the solar plexus, the first of seven "sacred impulses." If an image helped us to arouse wish, Bennett suggested the image of the "inner master." "I hope," "I believe," "I obey," "I love," and two further points, comprised the sequence.

The exercise roused an opposite impulse, of rebellion. I learned that I could indeed wish without wanting, but how was I supposed to hope without wanting? I saw how attached I was to my own slavery.

I was not alone in such self-revelations. A student spoke up in a meeting, saying that, after taking stock of his inner condition over the past months, trying to find sacred impulses in himself was "a real joke." Bennett recognized this sincere admission, but pointed out to the student that he was, as a result of his insight, stewing in self-pity.

The *"latifas,"* he explained, in spite of their having specific locations in the solar plexus, are really peepholes through which these high influences are asked to enter. It is beyond all of us, he said, to create hope and belief and love and obedience. But we can ask for such actions to come to us.

This uncompromising petition to higher powers was only the beginning of the exercise. From there forward it was as if help was an accomplished fact. Further, subtler barriers would be lifted. "If there were not such help," Bennett said again and again, "there would be no point in what we are trying to do here. It would be crazy."

"I obey" set off a palace revolution. A number of my little selves came forward and barricaded the exits. Under protest, "I" somehow followed the steps that Bennett led us through, adding a new one each morning. I felt most uncomfortable with myself, as if I belonged somewhere else. If ever I wanted a taste of Holy Denying, here it was. I wanted to go hide in the big anonymous outside world.

Underneath my squirming tantrums the exercise did its own work. I came to find I was capable of performing the steps with provisional sincerity, and this brought a kind of relief, as if this new work was an initiation. Bennett was not teaching a technique; he was showing us how to surrender to God.

LYNN O'BRIEN WAS keeping a journal around this time, in which she recorded a conversation with Bennett about the religious impulse, and the variety with which it affects people.

> Sunday, May 7, 1972. I went to Mass this morning with Mr. Bennett in his car. Coming back he asked me why I go to church. I told him people always thought of me as Catholic—the Irish name, and six brothers and sisters. Now I was wondering if Catholicism was my "objective religion."
>
> "Is that a good reason to go? Must not go in order to get out of work or because it is interesting."
>
> "I've found that I am receptive to this in a way I haven't been able to (be) before."
>
> "You must guard against this."
>
> "I don't understand. Do you mean guard against this feeling?"
>
> "Church is for people who need this. You must not go because it makes you feel good, or out of interest, or because you think God will love you more if you do this. Go with a sense of duty. You must have to go. Resist interest."
>
> I feel that he gave me a valuable piece of information. Why have I been going to church? Because: I am interested, I think it is good, I am vulnerable and want something concrete. I would be satisfied if I could have a religious conversion and thereby have something to hold on to when I leave here.

Anja Liengaard asked point blank if there was an afterlife. She was plagued by the nagging suspicion that the whole universe was really a meat grinder. He replied to her in no uncertain terms that there was, that he had seen it himself, and there was no doubt. It was what Anja needed to hear. She was in a perpetual argument with herself about the fairness of life, of eating anything in order to survive.

Bennett often cited his own moments of revelation as perfectly respectable source material. But one day he said something which was a droll comment on his culture: "All the work, this lifelong refinement of substances, coming to nothing, would be ... unacceptable." A friend of mine later commented, much amused, "Only the English would say that!"

CHAPTER ~ EIGHTEEN

IT IS SAID that we cannot see another person's work. But Sherborne was an intimate environment, putting us in regular contact with one another's inner states and manifestations.

I was seated next to Jane at a first-rate Chinese restaurant in Richmond. A dozen of us were guests of Diane, in return for helping her move her furniture and storage to a new London location. The appetizer was ordered a day in advance, a magnificent Peking duck. Many of us were on non-smoking regimes. I succumbed and borrowed a cigarette to top off the meal. Jane Cole was offered one, whereupon she became still, looking at her food.

Hats off to all people who have quit smoking. This is a struggle between divided impulses that everyone can relate to. This particular evening, however, was consecrated to Epicurean delight. The temptation to indulge in the beloved tobacco was out in force. Suddenly I felt a "bioelectric" current course up her body, while visually she remained motionless. She declined with a nod.

Another time, I felt the same emanation from Dick Holland. He was diabetic and needed to avoid certain foods, and would settle on the vegetarian version, if necessary. After many failures on the part of the rotating cooking teams to observe his simple needs, he burst into the kitchen in anger and set his plate before me. "Where is the chief cook?", he demanded. I confessed I was the responsible one and apologized for not remembering to prepare a meal he could eat.

We were standing together at the big wooden table. Dick did not reply; but I felt the same wave, which passed through Jane, now pass through him. His shoulders and face relaxed, at peace. I took note.

My favorite memory in this vein was of Bjorn Nillson, looking down at the work he had just bumbled, with half a dozen people involved in the project looking at him incredulously. He stood there in his poncho, smiling from ear to ear at us, and voiced with simple, unforced delight what all of us were secretly pondering: "Boy, now that was stupid!"

My own super-effort: I was compelled to do something, make a real effort; something that was simple and could be known to be done, something that stretched the limits way beyond anything I had done in my life. I remembered Bennett's story of digging in the garden at Fontainbleau and settled upon doing just that. I decided to dig the garden at high speed for forty-five minutes by my watch, enforced in the following way: whenever I felt myself slowing down, I would dig twice as fast, then level off to the established pace.

The dense clay soil of the kitchen garden was being prepared for potato planting in hundred-foot rows. I chose one that had been started, paused for a minute, and became a high-speed engine.

Forty-five minutes later, I sat, caught my breath and collected myself, then returned the shovel. My arms, the shovel, gravity itself, seemed to have little effect. I felt like a dynamo. I lay down in my room on my back and stared up at the ceiling, enjoying the boundless energy. At the next session, Bennett turned his smile on me and asked me what I had been doing. I was surprised by the question and asked what he meant. He said something had happened to me, he could tell. I asked, how? By your aura, he said. I explained the digging of the garden and the way it had been done. He said something else; he was very pleased and interested about this. While he was speaking I remembered his own Prieure experience, of his sudden ability to summon and feel any emotion at will, a state which lasted for hours. I reported that I did not notice such an ability to have arisen in me; for that matter I had not attempted to evoke any emotion at all, content as I was in my present state of well-being. He said this effort has important significance for me. He grinned off-handedly and added that, for breaking through to higher emotional center, I perhaps had not worked quite hard enough. This was not intended to, nor did it, temper my self-satisfaction. I felt like I had initiated myself into new life.

Since "B" seemed to see right into me, there were times when I avoided him like the plague. I was sure that all my impurities, my fantasies, my weaseling self-justifications, the buffers that get me through life, Bennett read in an instant. He knew or affected to know—probably a combination of both—where and how I stood that moment. He served as the stand-in for absentee conscience and lapsed aim. "Using me," he said, "or any authority figure as a surrogate will, is a stage you must go through, then get past. Many people never get past this point. But if the center of gravity of our work comes from our own wish, other work becomes possible."

Bennett described his role in our education with candor. "I remember a time when I came to seriously doubt this work. I could not see evidence in others or even in myself that we were really any different for having heard these ideas. I was in great distress, because I could not share this or speak of it: I had many people who were dependent on me and would be influenced by my personal doubts, and so kept all this to myself, wondering if it would pass. This lasted for almost two years."

He also revealed himself with even alarming candor. Late one night I was posted near a telephone, for after-hours house duty, to intercept an important call. Bennett came down in his robe to see if his call had come yet. He loomed from the darkness into the nimbus of my small lamp, and spoke to me with his shapeless maw. He had left a full set of uppers and lowers upstairs to soak. He looked old and weather-beaten and barely presentable and knew it, but without batting an eye was himself completely. A student, who attended the course the following year, tells me he delivered one of his lectures without his teeth, and without the coyest acknowledgment of anything being out of the usual.

"I *HATE* MR. BENNETT," Anne Claire said. Anne Claire, Sally and I were on a Sunday morning walk, along a footpath between fields of new spring growth fenced in stone. Anne Claire was about eleven, an age for trying out one's feelings and opinions on the world. "He is always better than everyone else. He works harder, knows more and does more than anyone else. Always, everybody is second compared to Mr. B."

Anne Claire had lived with her father, Dick Holland, at Coombe Springs. The children of both families were close. She had been observing the aging phenomenon, J.G. Bennett, for most of her life through her child's eyes. I was impressed first by her sensitivity toward other people and also for her acuity in targeting Bennett's character—that of the head honcho.

Had Bennett pursued a more conventional life, he probably would have been a CEO or MP. "People have asked me why, in spite of having abilities and so on, I have never made a success of my life. I asked myself this question very seriously. I asked what being a success means. From what I observed of people who are said to be a success, I became less interested in it as an objective. So I did not become one."

Low laughter from the group. Then, with a private wink, he said, "except in a private side-line." We received it with laughter. It was daringly egoistic of him. But I rather think he was saying, shake off false humility, own up to the fact that you are increased by your struggles and forebearances. Hide not your light under the bushel, as is said in "The Sermon on the Mount." At any rate, he justified his bravado by having made his time on earth count. "Mr. B never wastes a minute," Elizabeth said a second time. "Can you know what that means?"

BENNETT FREQUENTLY RETURNED to Gurdjieff's tale of the "Two Streams of Life," which says men and women end their earthly existence in the same way a drop of water in a dividing stream has two possible fates: to return to the great Father Ocean, where souls are delivered into new evolutions of growth; or to disappear into Mother Earth, to dissolve and be re-absorbed into the stuff out of which new life emerges. Along the way the streams are near each other, and at torrential places single drops sometimes change from one stream to the other.

"Which brings you all here?"

I record him, toward the end of the course, inserting into one of his talks a foreshadowing of our inevitable loss of will, for work and otherwise, which we must face after Sherborne.

July 7, 1972. When we leave this school, we will have a lawful reaction,

> resulting in the inability to work or lack of desire to work. Later the need to work comes again. We must try to remember what was said now. It is similar to a woman who has just had a baby, who has performed all her necessary functions automatically, with no need of conscious participation on her part. But after her adjustment back from pregnancy, the need to work returns. The ten month course of the Academy is necessarily attuned to the time it takes to prepare a baby- or fix the work inside oneself. Through us the work is born again and again into the world. When the time comes, the work is taken up with decision.

THE STUDENT, ROGER, whose humorous perspective on things I appreciated, suffered disillusionment with Bennett and the "work scene" in general. He suspected it was following the pattern of a movement, invariably attracting people wanting to belong to something. He knew the tendency was in himself, when he became politically active in college. At the Columbia student demonstrations, Roger discovered in himself a formidable oratory power for influencing crowds to action. He got hooked on the microphone, letting the swelling crowd of students egg him on to flights of unrehearsed rhetoric. He had the good sense to see through his low-budget rise to power. He wanted to have a mind and a heart and a soul and threw himself into work studies toward this end. But the hierarchical trappings, the timid novices and keepers of the flame, he found wanting. With Bennett he hoped things would be different. Bennett was an independent cuss, who wanted to bust the secrecy of the Fourth Way establishment wide open. Now, he thought, he could see a circle of acolytes gathering around Bennett instead.

We enjoyed speaking our minds to each other, which was natural for him. He told me he got a second opinion about his future involvement with Bennett, as it happened, from Pir Vilayat Inayat Khan, who was booked for appearances in London.

I told him what Bennett said when I asked him what he thought of the assertion that people—our own parents, for instance—who do not work on themselves in this life "perish like dogs." Bennett's answer was gloomy, as Roger predicted. While listening to this, it struck me that Roger might have been fishing for more ammunition to sunder his relationship.

When he told Pir Vilayat what Bennett had to say about it, Pir Vilayat just laughed: "My God! I thought the Calvinists had cornered that market!" This settled the issue for Roger. "I'll stick it out here, so as to leave nothing unfinished. But as far as I'm concerned, Allen, my advice to us all is, go for the money!" And he flashed his Jerry Garcia grin. I broke into laughter. We go through what we need to—each in our own way—I reasoned to myself.

As for Bennett's opinion that those who never worked on themselves died like dogs, he once told a story about a man he knew, who was "a Christmas tree of vices." The man got cancer and went through psychological and spiritual torment that was long and painful. "Yes," Bennett said, "he came to something by the end. There are many possibilities for man. But I wonder how many of us would choose to go through that door."

SO THERE WERE believers and unbelievers, it could be said. Bennett was an egoist with a mission; a saint with a mission; a fool with mission. I myself was a true blue believer, but a doubter as well. In terms of a learning process, the swings between belief and disbelief were simply material for observation. It did not matter what I thought, what people thought—about anything.

I could not help wonder how much of JGB was an impersonation. Had the impersonation become the impersonator? He himself seemed to embody his own paradoxical epithet when he was speaking about Sherborne House: "Sometimes a thing is disguised by appearing to be exactly what it is." That observation drew spontaneous applause from everyone in the room.

We students were simply taking in as much as we could of the course, hoping to digest some of it later. Like a roller coaster ride at the end of the last descent, we roar under a sign reading in big letters: "School's Out!" I would not begin learning anything until after Sherborne.

So we subsisted in a tranquil, elegant, almost palatial environment. Fresh food came in from our gardens, animals grew healthful and multiplied. Spring brought all the verdant dazzlement back after the long English winter. Summer cooked with life. Life was everywhere, clean and good, from one end of the green to the other. No car engines, no phones, no radios, no newspapers, no movies. An occasional outing to an abbey, a Norman cathedral, a wild bird preserve. Free on weekends to head out for the churches, pubs and restaurants of Tewkesbury, Northleach, Cirencester, Bourton-on-the-Water, the boutiques of Cheltenham and Gloucester.

The Holy Planet Purgatory is described by Beelzebub as a place of indescribable beauty, where every needful thing is provided in plenty, where the beatific vision comes frequently to comfort the anguished beings of that Planet, who, having seen and now yearn for unity with Our Endless Maker and Creator, must consciously endure their inevitable separation, until the last purification, before coming home to the Most Holy Sun Absolute. We too were surrounded by beauty everywhere. We feasted on the abundant energy, the days of silence, the fast days (dreadful as they were) and the simple graces, with some measure of humility and respect.

CHAPTER ~ NINETEEN

THE LAST AFTERNOON of my year at Sherborne I spent elsewhere. I chauffeured Dick Holland around on a couple of errands. We stopped for a pint in a village pub. He was amicable, enjoying the meandering conversation. In our open friendliness he shared anecdotes about days past among Coombe Springs society.

At once his face was serious, as if an inner weight reasserted itself. With hesitation, he told me about his wife, Anne Claire's, mother. He remarried late in life; she was considerably younger, and they were much in love. Then one day, while waving to each other through the rear window of an automobile carrying her away on a journey, both of their faces suddenly registered an undeniable premonition that they would never see each other again. He learned hours later that she was killed in the vehicle.

That was a fitting moment for finishing our pints and getting back on the road. His last errand took us to a small book store in the square of a distant village. The door opened onto a compact, but discerning, display of metaphysical literature. The proprietor and a patron recognized and greeted him. Mr. Holland introduced me as a graduate of J.G. Bennett's school at Sherborne House. "Ah," the proprietor said, "you must have gained some insight after that!" I imagined in his voice a tone of friendly jest, a hint of irony, but judging by his gaze there was none of either. Only his open wonderment. Not knowing what to say, beyond making a joke of it, I coughed up a laugh and stuck my nose in a book. Holland and the shopkeeper returned to their rather involved discussion about a printing order. I listened respectfully from a distance. Then we left.

That was my first encounter with a courteous inquiry about what I got from "the Sherborne course."

The afternoon was drawing late when we returned to the house. I thanked Dick for the pleasure of his company and went out past the orangery to join the others. A long firemound shimmered in the center of a semi-circle of benches borrowed from the dining room. One man basted large cuts of meat while another turned the spit. A gathering of deadwood lay in state for the night's bonfire. People moved about with glasses of cider and wine, admiring the serving tables laden with salads and side dishes. Late in the day the meat was removed from the spit and carved. Our last feast together commenced without ceremony; no speech or toast, no moment of silence. A general mood, of relief mixed with resignation, reigned over the affair as I remember it, a respectable show of joking, good cheer and midsummer drinking.

I refilled my glass and sat down in the circle again. On the far side of the firepit the cinder path bisected the visual field, beyond which a green embankment rose to eye-level—part of the original old forest, before the formal lawns and gardens were excavated. The modest promontory was shaded by great larches which stood like lords in waiting around their queen, a magnificent Lebanese cedar whose seed had been carried back from the Crusades.

To the right of this scene was the western facade of the house, its Corinthian columns and carved relief drenched in saffron sunset. Every part of this composition was so consummated as to be its own graven image. The cedar, of course, was larger than life: its lowest bough made a colossal proscenium over our performance of *Midsummer Night's Dream*. Puck swung in a sixty-foot arc under its airy, sculpted immensity, like a spider swinging from one sprig to another.

In one of the spontaneous conversations I took part in, a woman remarked that she knew the people at Sherborne better than she did members of her own family. The three or four of us nodded in agreement. But later I began to wonder how swiftly memory would render down these names and faces into a gelled still-life. Perhaps their imprints were already beginning their slow, lawful disintegration in my mind, the day before departure! In this knowledge I watched people practicing goodbyes, ranging from boisterous to solemn; forming and reforming in groups around the freshly stoked bonfire; carrying trays of food and tableware back to the kitchen. The last brilliant display of July sunset hailed a stark rising moon.

George Cornelius and I had a glass of beer together, walking and chatting. As we sat down in the circle of benches, he also turned to recounting fresh tales about Mr. Gurdjieff. George somehow had it arranged by Naval Intelligence for him to contact Gurdjieff, ostensibly to ascertain his possible connections with the Germans, the Vichy government, and/or the Bolsheviks. In reality he was helping Bennett and his people to forge connections with Gurdjieff and his Paris circle.

When George knocked on the door of 6 Rue des Colonels Rénard, a French-speaking woman answered. A male voice from the recesses was heard to ask who it was. "He wants to talk to you." "Ask him if he has any money," the voice said bluntly. George made no delay in seizing the moment: "I'm an American and, yes, I've brought plenty of money." That got him in the door.

It was a good story, which he followed with another one he was saving for last. Being part of Bennett's English retinue, George visited Gurdjieff several times, until he received orders for duty in eastern Turkey.

While there on a mission involving a radio transmitter on Ararat's slopes, he came down with a multiple infliction of jaundice, pneumonia, and dysentery. His fever rose precipitously. The army medical staff in Ankara was doubtful of his surviving the night. In the midst of delirium he saw Gurdjieff's photograph, which he requested be hung in his room.

George leaned forward and looked straight at me. "All of a sudden I heard him speaking. His voice sounded just like wind whistling in iced-up telephone lines in the winter—you ever hear that sound?—and said: 'Not worry, American, you not die.'"

George's delirium broke during the night. All he could remember of the past days was the vivid transcontinental reception of the voice. As soon as George was able, he returned to Paris to relate his unusual tale. Packed into Gurdjieff's apartment were the customary visitors and hangers-on, making private talk impossible. But he found himself seated next to him for the supper. The first words to him from Gurdjieff came abruptly, like a little thunderclap inserted between two moments: "You believe now, don't you, American? I say not die; not die."

The ghost of an old Transcaucasian sly man spread palpably over the evening.

George and I shook hands and wished each other well. He and Mary stayed on for some months, to assist Bennett in getting the second year under way, before returning to their home in Anchorage. George and Mary eventually moved to the lower forty and founded a work center in the wooded meadow valleys of Cave Junction, Oregon, where I found them again eighteen years later. There they continued to bring together isolated individuals and splintered work groups for work weekends and more ambitious seminars, such as staging original plays annually for the folk of Josephine County.

Someone else sat down next to me to talk for a while, during which I remembered a piece of unsubstantiated gossip I was suddenly inspired to pass on. Nobody's damned business, of course, but I couldn't resist. After tonight, who on earth would be interested in a story about any one of these people? "Ah!" I announced brightly, "I heard an interesting bit about Anna Durco!" I had his full attention. But just then someone, passing by, interrupted us to speak with my companion. I drank off my beer and looked about.

And there she was, seated not twenty feet to my left, with absolutely no one between us! How I had not been aware of her came to me as a complete shock, since I recalled seeing her in that very place during the supper. Her skill at containing herself in crowds was consummate. She could not have missed my blurted-out announcement, but she remained composed, looking straight ahead, no blinking, a scintilla of amusement projecting through her expression: as if she had heard nothing; as if she heard plainly and was not letting on.

That was my cue to withdraw. When my companion turned back to me to resume our conversation, I started off on another subject, hiding my squirming embarrassment. When he left to mix with the crowds, I found myself gazing at a lone tree at the opposite end of the green, losing itself in the background of the tall yews. Its low hem of foliage shrouded the stout trunk from view; a place to observe things, unnoticed.

Mr. Bennett passed by and noticed me there. He thrust out sideways his glass of wine to right himself, while bending his considerable height under the low hanging boughs. When his shoe found a foothold in the sprawling tree roots, he pivoted himself about-face and fell gently back against the trunk, beside me, not spilling a drop. He greeted me. We drank, both of us looking on in silence at the antics and small ceremonies of graduation night.

He got around rather quickly to asking what I was planning to do. I was not at all sure of what I was feeling that moment, a mix of calm and foreboding. I said I had been thinking of studying architecture, although I had not; but I then suddenly remembered that architecture was an old daydream of mine. Bennett thought for a minute about what I said. "Yes," he finally answered, "I can see you doing that." That moment, I felt like I was an unknown island suddenly being discovered by a passing ship. "I could send off a letter to Olgivanna Wright; perhaps she can do something for you. I have not been a favorite of hers: but, yes, you can bring her a letter from me." If I had decided to seek out Mrs. Wright at Taliesin, he surely would have written the letter within the day. But I did not seek her out. In fact, I eventually entered the architect's profession, but by a more circuitous path.

We chatted a bit more, and then he said, "I believe you have gotten this Work down into your bones. It will not abandon you, even when it seems that everything has flown away." He told me to keep him apprised of what I was doing. I told him I would do so. Together we stepped out from under the foliage, and walked off in different directions. I did not speak with Bennett again.

A FEW PEOPLE remained at Sherborne after the course ended, including my home-town friend, Eric Davis. Eric had gone through evident changes that year. His reserved and skeptical stance in life was not so evident. His initial reservations of the course were no longer a topic. Standing in Eric's room one day, I saw pinned above the writing desk, a strip of paper on which two words were penciled: *real understanding.* I surmised that some chord inside him had been struck, about which he communicated nothing. More and more regularly he remained seated alone in the ballroom after the late meditation.

One day I looked out of the library window and spied Bennett and Eric walking slowly together along the cinder path, heads down, immersed in talk. Clearly something was going on.

Eric and I were having another glass together when he said that he and Ann were staying on to help Bennett for a while. Again, no details.

Upon their return home six months later, Eric invited me to help him start a study group. I backed out of it at just about the last minute. He went ahead on his own steam and gathered about him a core group of a dozen people not much younger than himself, who returned faithfully whenever he convened a new round of meetings. Several of these people traveled to Claymont Court, near the Blue Ridge Mountains and Harper's Ferry, to help open the American branch of the Academy, in 1975, and enroll in the first American ten-month course.

Virgil Walker intended to stay on, and Bennett concurred. But a month after the course ended, Bennett told him it was time for him to leave. There was no arguing the matter; Virgil knew how blunt Bennett was when he chose to be. Back in spring, shortly after the night Virgil pushed his thumbs through the shot glass, he knocked on the door of Bennett's flat—wanting his help. It seemed he no longer knew who he was, that he had lost every mooring he ever had—his nationality, his beliefs, his marriage—smashed like a china vase. Bennett opened the door, saw the situation, beamed with delight and quietly shut the door in his face.

Virgil says of Bennett's handling of the situation: "It was not long afterward that I realized what he did was the kindest act anyone ever did for me. It would have been so easy for him, in his position, to use people for his own ends, to suck them dry. He certainly had the power to do it."

Apart from the few who stayed on for one reason or another, the rest of us were shown the door with the same finality. One hundred new students waited in the wings for the second basic course to begin; enrollment had been filled since mid-winter. The course would be somewhat different, after a dress rehearsal by the first year students, who were now history.

The next morning, most of us made hasty goodbyes and loaded ourselves into vehicles bound for London. The engine turned over, we actually were pulling away from the front door! We fell silent while the house and property, the magnificent canopy of venerable old trees, scrolled across the windows of Tim's van for the last time.

From a self-supporting environment that provided for all our needs, we stepped into the world of households, private sanctuaries, emotional fences, the ubiquitous reckonings about money. I was alarmed at how easily I refitted myself into the outside world, like an old coat.

NAME & SUBJECT ~ INDEX

Aga, 25
Alaska, 19-20
Allen, John, 67, 89-90
Alpert, Richard, 15
America's Boer War, 15
American Academy , 85
American Society, 95
Amsterdam, 6
Anderson, Paul and Naomi, 21
Ankara, 115
Aristotle, 11
attention, 11, 23, 30-33
    directing of, 31
awareness, 1, 31, 35-36, 39-40, 49, 92
awareness of material objects, 36

Bass, 90
Beelzebub's Tales to His Grandson, 4, 18, 22, 42
Benedictine Monastery, 15
Bennetron, 69
Bennett, Ben, 30
Bennett, Elizabeth, 7, 16, 36-37, 67, 88, 90, 99, 111
Bennett, Hero and Tessa, 37
Bennett, J. G., 1, 4-16, 18-23, 25-31, 33-37, 40, 42-54, 56, 63-70, 74-81, 83-84, 88-95, 97-108, 110-113, 115-118
Bhante, 5-6, 81, 84-87
Biosphere II, 90
Bjorn, 109
Blake, A. G. E., 9, 13, 88-90
Blum, Manfred, 44, 96
body is not material, 92, 104
Born, Max, 11
Bourton-on-the-Water, 113
British Intelligence, 10, 13
Buddha, 5, 85
Buddhism, 84

California, 84, 86
Canon of Seven, 74
Carnegie Hall, 80
Catholicism, 15, 107
Caucasians, 21
Chicago World Fair, 78
child care, 29, 37-39
Church of St. Germaine, 82
Claire, Anne, 111
Claymont Court, 85, 95, 117
Claymont School for Continuous Education, 85
compassionate idiot, 83
conscience, 22-23, 65, 73, 110
Coombe Springs, 3-7, 10, 12-14, 20, 26, 39, 42, 53, 70, 111, 114
Coombe Springs Press, 7, 53
Cornelius, George, 21, 69, 81, 115
Cornelius, Mary, 19, 70
Cotswold stone, 17
Cotswolds, 16, 90
creation, 34, 97

Daniel, Brent, 9
Davis, Ann, 21, 111, 114, 117
Davis, Eric, 21, 117
dervish, 12, 20, 44, 51, 73-75, 78-79
Dharmawara (Bhante), 5-6, 86
Djashkent, 79
Dramatic Universe, The, 11-12, 13, 21, 37, 88, 89, 97
Duffell, Richard, 20
Durco, Anna, 7, 9, 21, 39-41, 45, 68, 72, 77-80, 101, 116

ecstasy, 101
Edwards, Gilbert, 18
Eiffel Tower, 82
Elliot, Pierre, 9, 95
enneagram rose garden, 34-35
Essene Brotherhood, 74

feeling, 7, 22, 24, 27, 31, 45-47, 49, 53, 66, 75, 98, 100, 102, 107, 117

feeling apparatus, 46
First Obligatory, 7, 72
Fontainbleau, 109
Fort Worth, 90
Fourth Way, The, 7, 12-13, 15, 31, 46, 63, 112
Friends World College, 5

garden, 3, 20, 27, 33-35, 103, 109-110
gardening, 19, 28, 34, 36, 103
General Electric Company, 14
Georgetown, 85
Glastonbury, 15
Great Hall, The, 17-18
Greek Letters, 75
Green, Gerald, 75, 93
Gross, Jane, 86
Gurdjieff, 1, 4, 6, 8, 10-13, 20, 22, 42, 53, 55, 69-70, 73-75, 77-79, 96, 98, 115-116
Gurdjieff Foundation, The, 69
Gurdjieff Society. The, 12
Gurdjieff's Institute, 80
Gurdjieff's Prieuré, 21
Gurdjieff-Ouspensky, 1

Hamadani, Yusuf, 79
Hartmann, Thomas de, 80
Hartzog, Betty, 38
Helstenius, Lili, 32
Holland, Dick, 53, 109, 111, 114
Holy Denying, 107
Holy Planet Purgatory, 113

Identified, 75, 103
India, 3-5, 7, 21, 80, 84-85
Inner Circle of Humanity, 92
inner master
Intelligent Enneagram, The, 88
International Academy for Continuous Education, 1, 3, 7, 15, 94
Istanbul, 10, 12, 74

jazba, 101-102

Kent State, 101
Kingston-Upon-Thames, 7, 81
Kuchinsky, Saul, 14
kwajagan, 37

Labour Party, 10
latifas, 106
Laurie, 69, 102
Leary, Timothy, 15
Liengaard, Anja, 19, 108
love, 22, 53, 84, 106-107, 114

Malamati, 83
Masters of Wisdom, 37
maya, 97
McDonald, Ramsay, 10
Megalocosmos, 97
Mehrauli, 3, 5, 84
Midsummer Night's Dream, 115
Mormon, 105-106
morning exercise, 28, 30, 43-46, 95, 105
Most Holy Sun Absolute, 90, 113
movements, 7, 12-13, 18, 20-21, 29, 34, 39-42, 47, 68-69, 72-78, 80, 90, 100-101, 103
Mr. B, 20, 51, 111
music, 19, 40, 43, 47, 73-75, 79, 101

nature, 23, 28, 49, 51-52, 54, 71, 85, 97, 102
Naval Intelligence, 115
New Age, 123
nine-point exercise, 46-47
Notre Dame, 82
Nott, C.S., 80

O'Brien, Lynn, 9, 20, 67, 107
Our Creator Endlessness, 97
Ouspensky, P.D., 1, 10-11, 13

Page, Brian, 5-6
Pak Subuh, 12
Paul, 21
Paxton, Avis, 20
pianist, 40, 76
Pir Vilayat Inayat Khan, 112
Popoff, Irmis, 21
practical work, 36, 80
prayer, 15, 58, 66, 75, 84, 91
Prieure, 110
Purdy, Patrick, 86
Purgatory, 99, 113

Quakers, 19

Renato, 65
Robert, 21
Robin, 6-7
Roger, 67-69, 112
Romany, 77, 79

Sacre Coeur of Montmartre, 82
Salzmann, Madame de, 12, 80
Sanskrit, 79
second body, 98-99
sensation, 7, 32, 36, 41, 45-46, 49, 68, 89, 92
Series of Thirty-Nine, 74
sexual stimulation, 43
Shahada, The, 74
Sharon, 105
Sharsi Varsi, 75
Sherborne, Lord Charles, 16
Sherborne Academy, 1, 6
Sherborne Village, 16, 42-43, 65, 94
Shivapuri Baba, 103
Shoemaker, The, 74
spiritualism, 98
Sri Aurobindo, 84
St. Augustine, 63
St. Wandrille, 15
Steiner, Rudolph, 9
struggle between good and evil, 97
struggling, 46
Subud, 12, 37, 100
Sufi, 4, 13, 67, 79, 101
sufism, 21
Sushud, Hasan, 37, 44, 91-92, 102, 104
Sutton, Laurence, 81
Sutton, Michael, 3-6, 9, 17, 33, 43, 80, 85, 88
Systemaster, 14
Systematics, 11, 123
Taliesin, 80, 117
Tarkovsky, 89
Tashkent, 79
Tate Gallery, 20
Tessa, 37
Tewkesbury, 113
Thanksgiving, 53
Theater of All Possibilities, 67, 90
theme meetings, 49-51
themes, 49-51, 73
thoughts, 12, 41, 45-47, 50, 77
Twenty-One, 73
Unfinished Obligatory, 74

Venerable Dharmawara Mahathera, 86
Venerable Vira Dharmawara, 5
Vietnam, 32
Walker, Virgil, 9, 19, 105, 117
Wallace, Edith, 9
Weaver, The, 74
wellingtons, 33
Wilde, Gerald, 20, 101, 105
Wilkinson, John, 53
World War I, 20
World War II, 1, 10
Worthington's Ale, 81
Wright, Frank Lloyd, 80, 117
Wright, Iovanna, 80
Wright, Olgivanna, 80, 117

Yesevis, 79

Yogi, 44

Zervan, 13

FOR A CURRENT LIST OF
BOOKS BY J.G. BENNETT

in the USA
and all countries except England
contact

Bennett Books
PO Box 1553
Santa Fe, NM 87504

505 986-1428
Bennettbks@aol.com

in England
contact

Bennett & Luck
212 Upper St.
London N1 1RL

0171 226.3422

Thank You for Purchasing This Book.

Use this page to order directly from Bennett Books
and receive *free shipping* when your order is $60 or more.

Call or write for current catalog.
This "free shipping" offer is good only in the U.S. until June 8, 1999.

All titles are by J.G. Bennett except "Sherborne" by Allen Roth

quantity/title (paper, unless otherwise noted)	**Price**	**Extended**
__Creative Thinking	$12.00	________
__Creation	$15.00	________
__Dramatic Universe, The, 4 vols.	$120	________
__Sherborne: An Experiment (Roth), paper	$20.00	________
__Sherborne: limited cloth edition	$75.00	________
__Masters of Wisdom, The	$18.00	________
__Witness: The Story of a Search	$20.00	________
__Making a Soul	$14.00	________
__Deeper Man	$18.00	________
__Elementary Systematics	$13.00	________
__Gurdjieff: Making a New World	$18.00	________
__What Are We Living For?	$11.00	________
__How We Do Things, monograph	$6.00	________
__Hazard: The Risk of Realization	$11.00	________
__Hazard: The Risk of Realization (cloth)	$22.00	________
__Is There Life on Earth?	$13.00	________
__Needs of a New Age Community	$11.00	________
__Sacred Influences	$10.00	________
__Enneagram Studies	$9.00	________
__Gurdjieff: A Very Great Enigma	$10.00	________
__Sex	$9.00	________
__Talks on Beelzebub's Tales	$11.00	________
__Way To Be Free, The	$14.00	________
__Idiots in Paris	$11.00	________
__Long Pilgrimage	$14.00	________
__Transformation	$15.00	________
__Sevenfold Work	$14.00	________
__Intimations	$10.00	________
__Energies	$15.00	________
	Sub Total	________

If subtotal is less than $60 **add** $6.00 shipping & handling ________

Even if the subtotal is over $50 add $6.00 to subtotal
if you want the books sent UPS ________

- *Unless you add $6 for UPS books will be sent Bookpost.*
- *Bennett Books is not responsible for books sent bookpost.*

NM residents please add 6.25% sales tax ________

Total enclosed ________

Outside US, write for proforma invoice

Check or MO in $U.S. drawn on a U.S. bank only; payable to:
Bennett Books: P.O. Box 1553, Santa Fe, NM 87504

For information: 505 986-1428 voice/fax jtombb@aol.com / email

Name____

Address____

City__________________________State_____ ZIP_______________

Phone_____________________ Date ____________________

SH-1P